Praise for *The Business Model Innovation Factory*

"Saul understands the scale of change needed in our times and the ways to breakthrough innovation. The creative skills that will carry us there will come from design-centered approaches instead of traditional business ones."

—**John Maeda, President, Rhode Island School of Design and author, *The Laws of Simplicity***

"This is a timely and compelling book. It shows us a path in pursuit of a more powerful form of innovation that has been largely ignored by executives. We will continue to ignore it at our peril. This book shows us how to turn mounting pressure into expanding opportunities for value creation and value capture."

—**John Hagel, co-author of *The Power of Pull* and co-chairman of the Center for the Edge**

"Over the years Saul has brought together an amazing band of innovators to explore the nature, content, and direction of their work. Anybody interested in innovation has benefited enormously from his work. Now he presents us with what is certain to end up a well-thumbed 'bible' of innovation of all kinds. The world needs this book!"

—**Len Schlesinger, President, Babson College**

"Every year I look forward to attending Saul Kaplan's incredible Business Innovation Factory conference to learn more about creativity, innovation, and the wonderful art of storytelling. Now Saul is bringing together those stories plus all his real-world experience as a full-fledged entrepreneur, government policy-maker, and 'innovation junkie' to offer us the gift of a remarkable book. Saul is dead-on in saying that incremental innovation won't hack it in the twenty-first century. Every CEO needs a business model innovation factory."

—**Bruce Nussbaum, former Assistant Managing Editor, *Businessweek* and Professor of Innovation and Design at Parsons School of Design**

"In established corporations, disruption has been like the weather—incessantly discussed, never deployed. Now Saul Kaplan—plainspoken, practical, and pugnacious—documents the principles, the tools, and the stories that prove business model change can be part of an organization's repertoire. This is the handbook for those who will no longer settle for the incremental."

—Chris Myer, founder, Monitor Talent
and author, *Standing on the Sun*

"Forget episodic or incremental innovation. *The Business Model Innovation Factory* by Saul Kaplan shows how your future rests on business model innovation. Learn the 15 principles that are critical to success."

—Stephen Denning, author of *The Leader's Guide to Radical Management*

how to stay
relevant when the
world is changing

the
business
model
innovation
factory

saul kaplan

WILEY

John Wiley & Sons, Inc.

Published by John Wiley & Sons, Inc., Hoboken, New Jersey.
Published simultaneously in Canada.

For general information on our other products and services or for technical support, please contact our Customer Care Department within the United States at (800) 762-2974, outside the United States at (317) 572-3993 or fax (317) 572-4002.

Wiley publishes in a variety of print and electronic formats and by print-on-demand. Some material included with standard print versions of this book may not be included in e-books or in print-on-demand. If this book refers to media such as a CD or DVD that is not included in the version you purchased, you may download this material at http://booksupport.wiley.com. For more information about Wiley products, visit www.wiley.com.

ISBN 978-1-118-14956-0 (cloth); ISBN 978-1-118-22590-5 (ebk);
ISBN 978-1-118-23914-8 (ebk); ISBN 978-1-118-26389-1 (ebk)

Printed in the United States of America

10 9 8 7 6 5 4 3 2 1

To my wife Susan,
for encouraging this grateful innovation junkie

Contents

Acknowledgments

This book would not have been possible if it wasn't for the encouragement, insight, irreverence, and contributions of the entire Business Innovation Factory (BIF) team. As I write this everyone is waiting for a winning Power Ball ticket holder to step forward and claim a $336 million prize. I don't have the ticket. But even if I did I can honestly say that I would still gladly come to work every day at BIF. Our team of energetic, creative, and hardworking innovation junkies teach me what innovation really means every day. I am proud to be part of this incredible team and grateful that they humor me on this life-long journey to seek a better way. The lessons and insights in this book are really due to their efforts and great work. I'm just the messenger. My deepest gratitude to the BIF team:

Christine Costello
Tori Drew
Jeff Drury
Kara Dziobek
Christine Flanagan
James Hamar
Katherine Hypolite
Samantha Kowalczyk
Eli Stefanski

I am also grateful to the entire BIF community of innovation junkies from around the world. Over the years I have been inspired by your optimism and passion to try new approaches. You have taught this dinosaur many new tricks and exposed me to a knowledge flow that allows me to learn every day. If the goal is to get better faster, you shine a light on the path and provide the not-so-subtle nudge to dare to try. There are far too many of you to mention by name. There have been over 200 storytellers willing to share their personal transformation stories at our annual Collaborative Innovation Summit. Over 2,000 participants have attended the summit bringing inspiration, joy, and hope for a better future, and many thousands more connected through social media platforms that keep the innovation conversation active, vibrant, and relevant. We have a steep learning curve ahead of us, but you provide me with a powerful sense of optimism that together we can change the world.

—Saul Kaplan

Introduction

Sometimes tweaks aren't enough. Sometimes nothing short of reinventing yourself, your organization, or your community is called for. The beginning of the twenty-first century is one of those times. If anything is certain about the new millennium, it's the pace of change. New technology relentlessly hurdles into our lives. Ideas and practices travel around the world at Internet speed. Social media enables individuals to self-organize and reorganize in ways unimaginable in the twentieth century. We also live in anxious times marked by economic uncertainty, but one thing is clear: relevancy is more fleeting than ever. How to stay relevant in a changing and uncertain world is one of the most important questions of our time.

Thriving in the midst of today's frenetic pace of change requires a new set of approaches and tools. Incremental change may have been enough at the end of an industrial era marked by "me-too" products and services, process reengineering, best practices, benchmarks, and continuous improvement. We have built institutions that are far better at share taking than at market making. We have become really good at tweaks. There are tons of books, experts, and tools to help us make marginal improvements in the way things work today and to fight it out with existing competitors for one more share point. But how do we become market makers? Incremental change may be necessary but it isn't sufficient for the twenty-first century, which will be defined by next practices, disruptive technologies, market making, and transformation.

The Business Model Innovation Factory is a book for all leaders who recognize that incremental change isn't enough. It's a book about transformation. It doesn't matter what type or size of organization or community you lead or aspire to lead. It could be a for-profit or nonprofit company, a school, or a government agency. It could be a nation, state, or city, or maybe even an online community. Or maybe you are one of a growing number of free agents working across projects and networks. Regardless of organization type or leadership role, all leaders need to learn the art and practice of transformation to stay relevant in a changing world. The most exciting and best opportunities require entirely new business models or ways to create, deliver, and capture value. The challenge all leaders face is how to reinvent a business model while the entire organization is working hard pedaling the bicycle of the current one. The twenty-first century screams for transformation, not tweaks. *The Business Model Innovation Factory* is a book for transformers.

I was inspired to write this book after spending thirty-plus years as an innovation junkie with every imaginable black and blue mark that comes from being a diehard change agent. I have been a student and innovation practitioner across the public and private sector, industries, and disciplines. I have observed hundreds of organizations and thousands of innovators attempt to do transformational things and settle for doing incremental things. The patterns are clear and the need for business model innovation seems obvious. I wrote this book to share my experience and ideas on how you can create a business model innovation factory to stay relevant in a changing world. The book is organized in four parts:

Part I: What You Have Always Done Isn't Working Anymore
Part II: Connect, Inspire, Transform: 15 Business Model Innovation Principles
Part III: Creating a Business Model Innovation Factory
Part IV: Business Models Aren't Just for Business

The book's first part establishes the basic building blocks of a business model and makes the case that business model innovation is the new strategic imperative. The goal for all leaders is to avoid being "netflixed." If netflixed isn't a verb it should be! Blockbuster saw DVD technology and Netflix coming. The United States Postal Service saw e-mail coming. University presidents see online content and social media platforms changing the way students learn. Yet when faced with the obvious and growing threat of a disruptive competitor, organizations remain stuck in their current business models. It's amazing how few organizations can clearly articulate their business model. Can yours? If you ask any 10 people in your organization to describe your current business model, will the answers even be close? Most leaders know there are alternative and potentially better ways to create, deliver, and capture value but struggle with how to change their business models.

In the face of a serious disruptive threat most leaders do what they are comfortable with and know how to do—they strengthen and become even more entrenched in their current business models. They add new products and services to the current model, deploy technology to strengthen current capabilities, extend the current business model into new markets, and they try to create favorable laws and go to court to block new business models. These strategies may create value in the short-term but none of these efforts to strengthen existing business models are effective for long in the face of a disruptive competitor that is changing the way value is created, delivered, and captured through an entirely new business model. Disruption is now the norm instead of the exception.

Leaders could get away with blindly focusing on a single business model in the twentieth century, when business models rarely changed. Most industrial-era leaders never had to change their business model. One model worked throughout their entire careers. They could focus on improving their market position and competitiveness by making incremental improvements to the existing model. Disruptive threats were rare and could be safely ignored. Not so in the twenty-first century, when the half-life or longevity of a business model is decreasing. Business models just don't last as long as they used to. New players are rapidly emerging, enabled by disruptive technology, refusing to play by industrial-era rules.

Business model innovators aren't constrained by existing business models. Business model innovation is becoming the new strategic imperative for all organization leaders. But how do you transform a business model while still living in the current one?

The book's second part provides innovators with a set of actionable principles to guide business model innovation efforts. It provides 15 actionable principles based on the observations of this innovation junkie throughout a 30-year career—practicing innovation while meandering across industry, consulting, government, and nonprofit leadership roles, and the over eight years of work with an incredible team at the Business Innovation Factory (BIF), a nonprofit I founded and lead as its Chief Catalyst, focusing on enabling real-world labs for business model and systems-level transformation. I have had the privilege of connecting, convening, exploring, and creating with some of the most inspiring innovators on the planet, and the principles of business model innovation detailed in this book come from this wonderful innovation journey.

Fifteen business model innovation principles are organized into three main themes: Connect, Inspire, Transform. Business model innovation is a team sport. It's bigger than any one of us. It's a collaborative act and connections are key. It requires all of us to build stronger collaboration muscle. The best value-creating opportunities are in the gray areas between us. We must become more comfortable in the gray area and get much better connecting across silos, disciplines, and sectors. The most exciting new business models are networks connecting capabilities across boundaries.

Successful business model innovators are inspiration accelerators. People excel at and commit to what they are passionate about. Transformation can only happen when people are committed to the hard work of change. People must be inspired and emotionally vested in cocreating a new future. Without inspiration business model innovation doesn't happen. The path to inspiration is through storytelling, one of the most important tools for any business model innovator. It's the best way to create emotional connections to new business model concepts and innovations.

Sharing stories is how to create a network of passionate supporters that can help make new business model ideas a reality. We remember stories. We relate to stories and they compel us to action. A business model is the story of how value is created, delivered, and captured.

Transformation is hard. We have to make it easier by creating the conditions for ongoing experimentation. It's easy to sketch a new business model on the whiteboard. It's much harder to take the concept off of the whiteboard and put it in to the real world. We spend far too much time thinking and planning and nowhere near enough time experimenting in the real world to see what works. We need to try more stuff. We can't possibly know if a new business model idea will work sitting in a conference room. We have to create the conditions in the real world where we can do R&D for new business models. If we want to stay relevant in the twenty-first century we have to experiment all the time. Leading organizations will have several business model experiments going on at all times.

New business model ideas come not by looking through the lens of the current business model, but by learning how to look through the lens of the customer. Transformational business models must be designed around ways to improve the customer experience, not around ways to improve the performance of the current business model. Business model innovation starts by bringing the voice and experience of the end-user into the center of an iterative design process.

When woven together, these 15 business model innovation principles provide guidelines to enable entirely new ways to create, deliver, and capture value. They enable transformation.

The book's third part provides an implementation road map to create a business model innovation factory. It answers the key operational questions: How do you conduct R&D for new business models? How can your organization establish a business model innovation factory? Business model innovation is the new strategic imperative and yet most leaders say they don't have the organizational capability to design, prototype, and test new business models.

Innovation is a better way to deliver value. Innovation is different than invention. It's only an innovation when it has actually delivered value or solved a problem in the real world. Invention is great but it's just an input to innovation. Innovation is about delivering value and requires a business model. Business model innovation is about new ways to create, deliver, and capture value. Many new business models don't require any invention at all. Often new business models just combine and recombine existing technologies and capabilities in different ways to change how value is delivered.

The real trick is creating a business model innovation factory where technologies and capabilities can be remixed in new combinations to deliver value. The imperative is to do R&D for new business models. Not just concepts on a whiteboard or in a consulting deck, but R&D in the real world to explore the viability of a new business model in real market conditions. Not just tweaks of the current business model, but entirely new ways to create, deliver, and capture value. Organizations need a business model innovation factory to explore new business models unconstrained by the current one.

A successful business model innovation factory has the autonomy and resources to explore even those business models that might disrupt the current one. At the same time it's connected to the core business in order to access existing capabilities to enable and accelerate business model experimentation. Easier said than done! The practice of R&D to develop new products and technologies is well established. Most organizations know how to develop new products that can be commercialized by the current business model in order to create new top line revenue growth. The new imperative is to establish the capability to do R&D for new business models, even those that might disrupt the current one.

Important implementation questions addressed in this section of the book include: How do you organize, staff, and resource a business model innovation factory? How do you test new business models in the real world? How do you manage the inevitable organizational conflict between a business model innovation factory and the core business? How do you scale a promising business model and deal with the threat of cannibalization to your current business model?

The book's fourth part demonstrates that business model innovation isn't just for business. One of the biggest surprises from the time I spent working in the public sector is how strenuously social sector organizations resist the notion that they have a business model. Nonprofits, government agencies, social enterprises, schools, and nongovernmental organizations (NGOs) consistently proclaim that they aren't businesses, and therefore business rules don't apply. Well, I'm sorry to break the news, but if an organization has a viable way to create, deliver, and capture value, it has a business model. It doesn't matter whether an organization is in the public or private sector. It doesn't matter if it's a nonprofit or a for-profit enterprise. All organizations have a business model.

Nonprofit corporations may not be providing a financial return to investors or owners, but they still capture value to finance activities with contributions, grants, and service revenue. Social enterprises may be mission-driven, focused on delivering social impact versus a financial return on investment, but they still need a sustainable model to scale. Government agencies are financed by taxes, fees, and service revenue, but are still accountable to deliver citizen value at scale. The idea that business models are just for business is just wrong. Any organization that wants to be relevant, to deliver value at scale, and to sustain itself must clearly articulate and evolve its business model. And if an organization doesn't have a sustainable business model, its days are numbered.

Perhaps the most important reason for developing common business model innovation language across public, private, nonprofit, and for-profit sectors is that transforming our important social systems including education, health care, and energy will require networked business models that cut across sectors. We need new hybrid models that don't fit cleanly into today's convenient sector buckets. We already see for-profit social enterprises, nonprofits with for-profit divisions, and for-profit companies with social missions. Traditional sector lines are blurring. We're going to see every imaginable permutation and will have to get comfortable with more experimentation and ambiguity. Economic prosperity and solutions for our big social system challenges require business model innovation across sectors. All organization leaders must learn how to do R&D for new business models. Nonprofit, social enterprise, school, and government leaders aren't exempt. Business models aren't just for business.

It's a great time to be a business model innovator. This is the innovator's day. The good news is that during turbulent economic times everyone looks to innovators for new solutions. The bad news is that we have turned innovation into a buzzword. Everyone is an innovator and everything is an innovation. And of course when that happens no one and nothing is. We have to get below the buzzwords. *The Business Model Innovation Factory* is for all leaders who want to stay relevant in a changing world. It makes the case for business model innovation as the new strategic imperative, shows how organizations can reinvent themselves by doing ongoing R&D for new business models, and provides an implementation road map for all business model innovators who want to go from tweaks to transformation.

the
business
model
innovation
factory

What You Have Always Done Isn't Working Anymore

1 Don't Get Netflixed: Your Current Business Model Isn't Going to Last Much Longer

The nuclear industry measures how long a radioactive material will retain its potency by its half-life, which is the time it takes for the material to lose half of its radioactivity. For instance, the half-life of Uranium-235 is 700 million years. No wonder nuclear proliferation is so feared! During the industrial era the half-life of a business model has been measured in generations. Business models have always lasted a long time. Business models rarely changed and were handed down from generation to generation. Most business leaders have never had to change their business model. Most CEOs have led a single business model throughout their entire career. They never learned how to change a business model in business school or from their peers, who also have never had to change their business models.

During the industrial era once the basic rules for how a company creates, delivers, and captures value were established they became etched in stone, fortified by functional silos, and sustained by reinforcing company cultures. All of a company's DNA, energy, and resources were focused on scaling the business model and beating back competition attempting to do a better job executing the same business model. Companies with nearly identical business models slugged it out for market share within well-defined industry sectors.

There was a mad rush to copy so-called best practices in order to not be left behind by industry leaders.

It should be no surprise that if you ask executives and corporate employees to define the term business model and to share their company's business model story you tend to get a lot of blank stares and very different stories from across the organization. For most, their business model has probably been in place since the business was started—before most employees joined the company. It hasn't changed. It is implicit. No one talks about it. No one shares business model stories because they are taken for granted.

Industry definitions are also taken for granted. As if industries were clubs with exclusive admission criteria and secret handshakes only revealed to companies that agree to play by understood rules. The industrial era has been defined by clearly delineated industries, making it easy to identify which sector every company is competing in. It was all so gentlemanly, as if competition was governed like boxing by a code of generally accepted Marquess of Queensberry rules. Companies were all conveniently assigned a numerical Standard Industrial Classification (SIC) code (now North American Industry Classification System, or NAICS) identifying which industry sector they fit into. Within each industry sector companies all migrated toward an identical business model competing for market share within the sector. Business models rarely changed.

Those days are over. The industrial era is not coming back. The half-life of a business model is declining. Business models just don't last as long as they used to. In the twenty-first century business leaders are unlikely to manage a single business model for an entire career. Business leaders are unlikely to hand down their businesses to the next generation of leaders with the same business model they inherited from the generation before. Leaders are either going to learn how to change their business models while pedaling the bicycle of the current one or they are going to be netflixed. The challenge in the twenty-first century for all leaders is how to avoid being netflixed.

If netflixed isn't a verb it should be.

netflix; netflixed
verb
1. to cause disruption or turmoil to an existing business model
2. to destroy a previously successful business model
3. to displace the way value is currently created, delivered, and captured
4. to be disrupted, destroyed, or displaced by a new business model

Blockbuster Gets Netflixed

Blockbuster started out with a compelling business model. Its value proposition was clear—enabling consumers to watch hit movies in the comfort of their homes. Blockbuster established an extensive value delivery network with stores conveniently located on every corner. Its first store opened in 1985 and it quickly grew to have over 5,000 retail outlets and 60,000 employees. It also had a smart financing model to capture value. It rented hit movies at a price consumers found attractive relative to the price of going out to the movies. Instead of paying a large upfront fee to buy videos from the studio (up to $65 per video) Blockbuster entered into a revenue-sharing model with the movie studios including little to no upfront costs per video, which gave them a huge advantage, and fueled explosive growth. Blockbuster started out on a roll. At its peak in 2002 Blockbuster's market cap rose to $5 billion. In 2010 it filed for bankruptcy. So what happened? Blockbuster was netflixed.

It wasn't as if Blockbuster didn't see Netflix coming. They were just so committed to their bricks and mortar business model they couldn't see or act beyond it. They were stuck in their business model. It became a straitjacket that eventually took the company down. You didn't have to be a fly on the wall of Blockbuster's headquarters during those years to imagine the management debate that took place on what to do about the emerging competitive upstart, Netflix.

As is often the case, the Blockbuster business model story starts and ends with technology playing a leading role. Initially, technology enabled and then ultimately disrupted Blockbuster's business model.

Early versions of the videocassette recorder (VCR) first appeared in the late 1950s and through the 1960s, but it wasn't until the late 1970s that they began to have any mass consumer market success. Who doesn't remember the great format war between Sony's Betamax and JVC's VHS competing videocassette standards? VHS won out due to a longer two-hour recording time with the ability to extend the recording time up to four hours. The last obstacle to broad consumer uptake of VCRs was overcoming the resistance of movie studios. Like any industry facing a business model threat, whether real or imagined, the movie industry fought hard to block the spread of VCR technology. Jack Valenti, head of the Motion Picture Association of America, implored Congress to protect the movie industry from the "savagery and the ravages of this machine." In Congressional testimony Valenti said, "the VCR is to the American film producer and the American public as the Boston strangler is to the woman home alone."[1] The case went all the way to the Supreme Court ruling in *Sony Corp. of America v. Universal City Studios, Inc.* that VCRs were allowable for private use. Ironically the movie industry ended up finding a significant new revenue source by distributing video recordings of their movies.

With consumer acceptance of VCRs expanding after the favorable Supreme Court ruling in 1984, Blockbuster opened its first store on October 1985 in Dallas, Texas, and never looked back, or over its shoulder, for that matter. Wayne Huizinga saw the potential to scale Blockbuster nationally, as he had previously done with garbage collection at Waste Management, and bought the company in 1987,

---

[1] From Jack Valenti testimony on April 12, 1982, before the Subcommittee on Courts, Civil Liberties, and the Administration of Justice of the Committee on the Judiciary House of Representatives on "Home Recording of Copyrighted Works."

starting with a few stores and quickly expanding through acquisitions and new store openings to become the largest retail video chain in the United States. In 1994 Huizinga sold Blockbuster to Viacom for $8.4 billion.

How smart was Huizinga, because in 1995 the DVD was invented. It was inevitable and easy to see. During the same period (in the late 1980s and early 1990s) that Blockbuster was capitalizing on consumer acceptance and demand for video recordings of hit movies, the demand for CD music recordings was also exploding. In 1982, Billy Joel's *52nd Street* was the first record album released on CD in Japan, where Sony also launched its first CD player. In 1983 CD players were commercialized in the United States, along with 16 CDs released from CBS records. By 1988, 400 million CDs were manufactured in 50 plants around the world.

It was only a matter of time until the same optical disc storage technology enabling CDs to displace vinyl records would also displace videocassette recordings of movies. It happened in 1995 with the invention of DVDs, which had the storage capacity for an entire feature length movie. DVDs quickly gained consumer acceptance in the market over videocassettes. DVDs offered higher quality, more durability, and introduced an attractive interactivity feature allowing viewers to go directly to chosen scenes within a movie. As the price of DVD players quickly came down in the market, DVDs soon became the favored home movie format.

Blockbuster didn't see the emergence of DVD technology as a threat to their business model. They didn't see it as a disruptive technology. They saw DVDs as a sustaining technology to improve the performance of their current bricks and mortar business model. DVDs would sit alongside videocassettes and be just another product offering to their retail customers. Blockbuster didn't see DVD technology as a possible enabler of new business models or ways to change the way they created, delivered, and captured customer value. That all changed in 1997, when Reed Hastings got pissed off because he was charged a late fee by Blockbuster after failing to return the movie *Apollo 13* within the due date. Turns out, Reed

Hastings was not alone in hating to pay Blockbuster's late fees. While consumers had no convenient alternative to renting movies from Blockbuster, the company extracted over $500 million in late fees from customers like Hastings. Blockbuster was so focused on expanding its current business model it had no clue it was about to be netflixed.

Netflix didn't invent any new technology. DVD optical disc storage technology had already been invented. What Netflix invented was a new business model. Netflix recognized that DVDs were small and light enough to mail using first-class postage. Netflix thought it could trump Blockbuster's value proposition, enabling consumers to watch hit movies in the comfort of their home by delivering movies directly to a customer's home by mail, allowing them to avoid a trip to the corner store. Initially, the rest of Netflix's business model was identical to Blockbuster's. In the beginning Netflix captured value in the same way as Blockbuster with a pay-per-rental pricing model. The only difference was the ability to order a movie online and have it delivered directly to your home by mail. The original Netflix business model even had the same late fee as Blockbuster for not returning the movie on time. Uptake was slow initially as people preferred the convenience of renting and watching a movie at the last minute without waiting for it to come by mail. Blockbuster initially saw Netflix as a niche mail order business that didn't represent a significant competitive threat.

That all changed when Netflix introduced its real business model innovation. In 1999 Netflix moved away from Blockbuster's pay-per-rental model and introduced a subscription model where customers paid a flat fee for unlimited rentals without due dates, late fees, or shipping and handling fees. Netflix's business model story was to enable consumers to watch as many movies as they wanted in the comfort of their home for a fixed monthly price. The new business model caught fire, with annual sales going from $1 million to $5 million in its first year. Within five years Netflix was a $500 million business and within eight years it had reached $1 billion in sales. In 2002 Netflix had 1 million subscribers, growing to over

5 million in 2006 and over 14 million in 2010. Hardly a niche business!

So did Blockbuster see Netflix coming? Did senior management see the opportunity to think beyond its bricks and mortar network expansion and store operations to deliver customer value in new ways? Did management see the disruptive potential of DVDs? Did they see Netflix coming and decide to stick with their bricks and mortar approach? Or did they just miss the opportunity because they were so busy pedaling the bicycle of their current business model they didn't think about and experiment with potential new ones?

I think the evidence is clear: Blockbuster saw Netflix coming and chose to ignore them at first and then reacted way too slowly. You may be surprised to learn that Blockbuster had the opportunity to partner with Netflix before the upstart really took off. John Antico, Blockbuster CEO, actually received a visit from Netflix founders Reed Hastings and Marc Randolf in 2000. The founders traveled to Blockboster's headquarters in Dallas to deliver an interesting offer to Antico. According to Barry McCarthy (Netflix CFO at the time), who joined Hastings and Randolf on the trip, the founders proposed that Netflix and Blockbuster collaborate. In an interview with The Unofficial Stanford Blog, McCarthy recounted the meeting saying, "Reed had the chutzpah to propose to them that we run their brand online and they run our brand in the stores and they just about laughed us out of their office. At least initially, they thought we were a very small niche business. Gradually over time, as we grew our market, his thinking evolved but initially they ignored us and that was much to our advantage."[2]

Blockbuster made the mistake most companies make in underestimating the disruptive threat of new technologies and innovative business models until it is too late. Blockbuster remained stuck in their bricks and mortar business model, naively treating Netflix as a niche player that they could ignore. They underestimated Netflix at

---

[2] See http://tusb.stanford.edu/2008/01/barry_mccarthy_chief_financial.html.

their own peril. They attempted to react, but it was too late. The constraints and pressures of their existing business model proved too great to overcome. Blockbuster was netflixed.

As Netflix took off and began to look like more than a niche competitor to Blockbuster CEO John Antico, he began to push very hard to respond to the threat with significant investment in an online platform and offering of Blockbuster's own called Total Access. The new platform, with direct attention from the CEO and resources to grow, gave Blockbuster a credible offering to counter Netflix. Antico's move was late but may have worked given Blockbuster's considerable resources, strategic relationships with movie producers, brand recognition, and substantial market share. But Antico ran directly into a conflict with none other than Blockbuster investor Carl Icahn. In 2004 Icahn took a significant ownership position, owning 11.5 million shares (or about 9.6 percent) of the company. Icahn wanted Antico and the company to ignore Netflix and continue to scale its bricks and mortar business model, adding more stores to the network. Icahn was upset with Antico and was publicly critical about his focus and investment in an online platform. Icahn won, convincing the board to replace Antico as CEO.

Any hope of changing Blockbuster's business model left with Antico and the company proceeded to stick with its bricks and mortar business model. That strategy proved disastrous to Blockbuster. The company went on to lose billions of dollars in shareholder value and ultimately filed for bankruptcy in 2010.

Even Netflix Is in Danger of Being Netflixed

The Blockbuster story is about a business model that was successful until a disruptive technology and a new business model displaced it. The story isn't unique to Blockbuster. All business models are vulnerable to being netflixed. Even Netflix has to worry about being netflixed.

Netflix is vulnerable to being netflixed on multiple fronts. They could be netflixed by a company like Redbox that distributes DVDs through a kiosk distribution model. Started in 2003 with rapid growth, Redbox had more retail outlets than Blockbuster by 2007. The cost to place and operate a Redbox kiosk is significantly less than the costs associated with operating a retail video store. It is also less than the cost of operating a mail fulfillment operation like the one Netflix operates. Redbox can rent a DVD from its kiosk network for $1 per-night, significantly less than both Blockbuster and Netflix are able to offer.

Of course the biggest threat of disruption to Netflix's business model comes from the ability to download or watch movies directly online. As broadband capacity becomes more ubiquitous it is now possible to watch movies on demand directly on the web. It is only a matter of time until both videocassettes and DVDs seem like an antiquated way to access digital video content. Netflix has been aggressively evolving its business model, experimenting with new online movie offerings and pricing models. It remains to be seen if Netflix can avoid being netflixed itself. It will face competition not only from traditional movie rental companies but also directly from movie producers and other media companies that can now directly distribute their content to consumers without needing capital intensive distribution channels.

Netflix initially tried to bundle streaming as a new product offering within its current business model. For customers that wanted to access movies through both the mail and online streaming, it offered a popular pricing plan of unlimited streaming and one movie out by mail at a time for $9.99 a month. Many liked the offer but with increasing costs it wasn't a sustainable proposition for Netflix. The growing cost of streaming rights and the increasing costs for bandwidth, infrastructure, and support to make streaming available were making a one low price per month for unlimited streaming and DVD delivery untenable for Netflix. Without the cash to gain streaming rights for popular content, Netflix would not be able to please customers interested in streaming. And of course customers who were only interested in a low price mail delivery model had no interest in paying higher prices for real time movie streaming. Something had to give.

Netflix announced a whopper of a price increase to all of its customers in July of 2011. They decided to get rid of the $9.99 bundled price plan and to separate the two offerings, each priced individually at $7.99. It was a 60 percent price increase and customer reaction was immediate and angry. Blog posts and comments piled up across the web in reaction and over a million customers voted with their feet by unsubscribing to the Netflix service. The business model that had worked so well for the DVD-by-mail service did not work well to deliver online streaming bundled with the mail service.

Netflix was seeing attacks from all angles. Sensing weakness, both Amazon and Wal-Mart stepped up their streaming offerings. Amazon closed deals with both Universal Pictures (1,000 movies) and CBS (2,000 episodes of popular TV shows) to increase the number of streaming offerings in its Amazon Prime library. Wal-Mart integrated its acquisition of Vudu, an online streaming service, under its online umbrella. Wal-Mart doesn't offer an unlimited monthly streaming service, but instead offers movies ranging in price from $1.00 to $5.99. Netflix's business model was under siege.

It only took two months for Netflix's next move. In September of 2011 it decided to split up into two discreet business units. One for online streaming continuing to operate under the name Netflix and another independent business unit established under the new name Quikster to operate the company's legacy DVD-by-mail service. It became clear to Netflix that trying to grow the streaming business within the core DVD-by-mail business model wouldn't work. If they were going to thrive in the streaming market it would require a different business model, a model with a unique way to create, deliver, and capture value. While it was going to remain a wholly owned subsidiary of the parent company, Netflix, it was to have the autonomy to continue to serve those customers that value its DVD-by-mail services. Alternatively, Netflix as part of this strategy would move quickly to leverage its leadership position in the streaming market in the face of significant competition.

In a blog post personally communicating the rationale for the business model changes at Netflix, CEO Reed Hastings provides wonderful insight into the mind-set of a CEO realizing his company is being netflixed. Hastings said, "we realized that streaming and DVD by mail are becoming two quite different businesses, with very different cost structures, different benefits that need to be marketed differently, and we need to let each grow and operate independently. It's hard for me to write this after over 10 years of mailing DVDs with pride."[3]

The most important lesson for all leaders to take away from Reed Hastings' experience at Netflix is from his simple but profound admission, "In hindsight, I slid into arrogance based upon past success." Hastings goes on to say in his blog post,

> My greatest fear at Netflix has been that we wouldn't make the leap from success in DVDs to success in streaming. Most companies that are great at something—like AOL dialup or Borders bookstores—do not become great at new things people want (streaming for us) because they are afraid to hurt their initial business. Eventually these companies realize their error of not focusing enough on the new thing, and then the company fights desperately and hopelessly to recover. Companies rarely die from moving too fast, and they frequently die from moving too slowly.

And then less than a month later, after losing over 1 million customers and the bleeding continuing, Reed Hastings announced Netflix had changed its mind again and would not be going forward with a separate Quikster business model and unit. They would continue to blend the online and DVD-by-mail offerings and pricing. He amazingly contradicted his comment that companies rarely die

---

[3] See http://blog.netflix.com/2011/09/explanation-and-some-reflections.html.

from moving too fast in his announcement saying, "Consumers value the simplicity Netflix has always offered and we respect that. There is a difference between moving quickly—which Netflix has done very well for years—and moving too fast, which is what we did in this case." It was painful to hear and to watch Netflix in the throes of being netflixed. At the time of this writing, it isn't clear how the movie will end, but it is clear that Netflix waited way too long to react to the disruptive potential of streaming and its schizophrenic actions have cost it significant customer loyalty and shareholder wealth. Stay tuned.

Here are a few other well-known examples of organizations that either have been or in the process of being netflixed:

Amazon netflixing Borders
Apple netflixing Tower Records
E-mail netflixing the United States Postal Service
Craigslist netflixing local newspapers
Google netflixing encyclopedias and libraries
Online education netflixing universities
Peapod netflixing grocery stores

How vulnerable is your business model to being netflixed?

Business models just don't last as long as they used to. They are all vulnerable to being netflixed. No one and no organization are immune. But how can you become the disrupter instead of the disrupted? Could Blockbuster or any company with a successful business model proactively work on entirely new business models simultaneously to improving the performance of the current one? I think the answer is yes, and the solution is to create a business model innovation factory where technologies and capabilities can be combined and recombined in new ways to deliver value unconstrained by the current business model.

Think Apple. Imagine the day in 1999 when Steve Jobs came in to work and told senior management the company was going to open up its own stores to sell Apple products directly to the consumer.

Everyone in the organization at that time was vested in a business model where products were distributed and sold only through authorized retailers like Sears and CompUSA. All of Apple's capabilities were aligned with this authorized retailer go-to-market model. No one at Apple had any direct-to-consumer retail experience. All of the management job descriptions, performance management systems, and incentive programs were geared toward supporting Apple's authorized retailer network. The entire financial control and measurement process supported the existing business model. Everyone must have seen any plan to open Apple stores as disruptive and a direct competitive threat to the way they did business. Not Steve Jobs. He wanted more direct control over the customer sales experience.

In a typical Jobs flourish he told *Fortune* magazine, "We have to do something, or we're going to be a victim of the plate tectonics. And we have to think different about this. We have to innovate here."[4] In January of 2000 Jobs hired Ron Johnson, who was then the vice president of retailing for Target, to lead the Apple direct retailing effort. Johnson led an internal project to design what is now the centerpiece of Apple's retail and customer experience strategy. At the time Apple only had two laptops and two desktop products to sell. There was no iPod or iPad yet. Instead of designing a traditional product purchasing experience into the retail space Johnson and his team designed an ownership experience, opening up the space to allow Genius Bars, training, and intimate customer service. The first store opened in 2001 in Virginia and by 2011 there were over 350 stores with premier locations around the world. It is hard to imagine Apple today without its compelling stores and customer experience, but unless Steve Jobs was willing to experiment with a new disruptive business model it would never have happened. In Johnson's own words, when he first arrived at Apple, "people thought I was crazy."

---

[4] "How Apple Became the Best Retailer in America," *Fortune*, March 8, 2007.

It is not unusual for people vested in any business model to view new business models and the people associated with designing them as crazy. The leadership challenge is how to keep the current business model performing while simultaneously experimenting with new ones even if they and the people deployed to working on them seem a little crazy at first.

To avoid being netflixed all leaders and organizations must learn how to do R&D for new business models. A successful business model innovation factory moves new ideas quickly from concepts doodled on a whiteboard to real world experiments to explore the viability of a new business model in real market conditions. These are not incremental changes to the current business model but entirely new ways to create, deliver, and capture value. Organizations need a business model innovation factory to explore new business models unconstrained by the current one.

A successful business model innovation factory has the freedom and access to the resources it needs to explore even those business models that might disrupt the current one. It also maintains a strong connection to the core business so it can access the capabilities it needs to accelerate business model experiments. Most organizations know how to do R&D to develop new products and technologies to drive top line revenue growth of the current business model. What organizations need to do that they aren't doing now is establish an ongoing R&D capability for new business models.

Before you can create a business model innovation factory the first step is to understand the basic components of a business model and to clearly articulate and map your current business model.

2 Business Models 101: Creating, Delivering, and Capturing Value

I will never forget the kickoff meeting of a project I led back in 1995 while a partner at the consulting firm Accenture to help the pharmaceutical company G.D. Searle & Co. improve its competitive market position. Richard De Schutter had been named the company's CEO that year and he wanted us to work with his new leadership team to break down long-standing functional silos within the organization. At our very first team meeting, De Schutter declared that the official language of the project was going to be English. He said "consultantese" was not permissible! Imagine our dilemma when we were told we couldn't speak in our native tongue or rely on jargon that only consultants can understand. And so "plain speak" became the project team mantra. De Schutter's admonition has stuck with me over the years. However tempting it is to revert to speaking consultantese, using understandable language is essential to advancing new ideas and compelling action. I have been in too many meetings over the years about business models and business model innovation where participants' eyes glaze over due to overly academic language and frameworks. If, as this book asserts, business model innovation is the new strategic imperative for all leaders, we must start by getting below the buzzwords. So in plain English, what the heck is a business model?

A business model is a story about how an organization creates, delivers, and captures value.

It isn't any more complicated than that. And yet if you ask 10 random leaders to define "business model" their answers are all over the place. Even worse, if you ask 10 people within the same organization to share the story of their current business model you will get blank stares and 10 different stories. Before any organization can begin thinking about business model innovation it must start by creating a collective understanding of what a business model is and a shared story of how the organization currently creates, delivers, and captures value. (See Figure 2.1.)

The story of your current business model can be constructed by answering three basic questions:

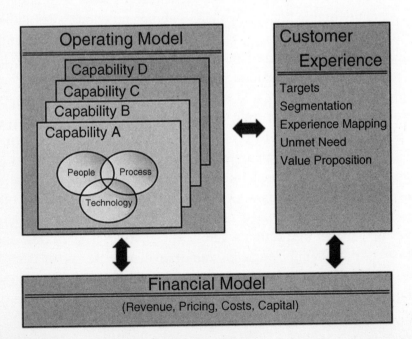

FIGURE 2.1 Business Model Elements

1. How does your organization create value?
2. How does your organization deliver value?
3. How does your organization capture value?

Let's examine each of the three business model story elements.

How Does Your Company Create Value?

Business models are designed to create value for a customer or end-user. The logical place to start in telling any business model story is to clearly articulate how the model creates value and for whom. What problem does the business model solve? What unmet market need does it fill? What compelling customer experience does it create? What promise of value do you make to your customers? One of my favorite ways to describe how a business model creates value is by first answering the question, what is the job the customer is hiring your company, product, or service to do?

Marketing guru and Harvard Business School (HBS) professor Theodore Levitt first introduced us to the jobs-to-be-done approach to define a company's value proposition. He famously proclaimed in 1975, "People don't want a quarter-inch drill, they want a quarter-inch hole." Levitt taught us value is in the eye of the customer and companies should define how they create value in the context of customer needs and problem solving. Innovation expert and HBS professor Clayton Christensen has been a consistent advocate for using a jobs-to-be-done approach to initiate any innovation process. Christensen and the consulting team at the firm he founded, Innosight, kick off innovation engagements by having clients answer the basic question, what fundamental problem is your customer trying to solve?

In his MBA class and outside speaking engagements Christensen drives home the importance of developing a deep understanding of the jobs customers are trying to do to shape every value proposition. He brings the jobs-to-be-done idea to life by sharing the story of a restaurant chain that wants to sell more milkshakes. The restaurant chain did extensive market research and segmented the milkshake market every imaginable way. They tried segmenting the market by product characteristic and by customer demographic with no success. They then began to look at the milkshake market not through the lens of the company but through the lens of the customer. The key question was, what job were customers hiring a milkshake to do? The answer surprised the company. It turned out 40 percent of the milkshakes were bought to-go by commuters first thing in the morning.

By closely observing customers it became clear that they were hiring the milkshake to last for their entire boring commute. They weren't hiring the milkshake instead of another drink. The milkshake was a substitute for a bagel or a doughnut. It was less messy and lasted for the entire commute. Armed with a new perspective gained only by deeply understanding the job that the customer was hiring a milkshake for the company could then improve both the product and its value proposition. Milkshake sales went up.

Another powerful example of using a jobs-to-be-done approach is by Whitney Johnson, founding partner of Rose Park Advisors, who in a Harvard Business Review (HBR) blog post clearly articulated the jobs she is hiring social media to do (see Figure 2.2). Companies in the social media business and those developing new social media platforms would do well to pay attention when Johnson describes the four reasons she is hiring various social media platforms. All companies should have this kind of clarity about the jobs customers are hiring their products and services for.

Jobs-to-Be-Done	Social Media Platform Hired
Help me find my voice and get published.	Personal blog and HBR
Help me be found professionally.	LinkedIn
Help me stay in touch with people I like even though our lives don't currently intersect.	Facebook
Help me expand my network.	Twitter

FIGURE 2.2 What Job Does Social Media Do For You?

Johnson is honest in admitting she also hires Twitter to help her procrastinate! I can relate. You can see what I mean by connecting with Whitney on Twitter at @JohnsonWhitney and with me at @skap5.

Understanding value through the lens of your customers is the best way to create a compelling value proposition. Your value proposition should be short, easily understood, and consistently shared by stakeholders both in and out of the company. Here are a few well-known examples of strong and clear value propositions. How does your organization currently create value?

- Angie's List: Reviews you can trust
- WalMart: Every day low prices
- BMW: The ultimate driving machine
- Zappos: Powered by service
- WholeFoods: Selling the highest quality natural and organic products
- IBM: Let's build a smarter planet
- Google: Organize the world's information and make it universally accessible and useful

How Does Your Organization Deliver Value?

Once you can clearly articulate a compelling value proposition, the next element of your business model story is about how the organization actually delivers the value it has promised to the market. It's one thing to have a compelling concept for creating value and quite another to deliver promised value consistently, with high quality, and at scale. This second element of a business model story describes how an organization goes about the work of delivering value. It is a description or picture of how the organization operates. It is an understandable way to describe your company's operating vision or operating model.

An operating model highlights capabilities deployed to deliver on a company's value proposition or promise to its customers. An operating model is not an organization chart. Operating models describe core capabilities and how they relate to each other; not only those capabilities within the four walls of the organization, but also capabilities from partner organizations that contribute to how value is delivered to customers.

I spent over 20 years as a road-warrior strategy consultant asking hundreds of executive teams to describe how their companies operated to deliver value to their customers. In almost every case they would start by telling me how they organized and handing me their organization charts. Organization charts do a great job of depicting reporting relationships and functional hierarchies but they do not provide a good sense of how work flows through a company across functions to deliver value. An organization chart does not tell the story of how the real work of an organization is done to deliver customer value. Organization charts do not show how teams form across functions to implement the core processes of the operation. They do not show which processes are key to delivering value to the customer. They do not show how functions relate to each other or how people, information, and resources flow through the organization. Organization charts also don't show how outside collaborators connect to support key parts of the value delivery process. In short, organization charts are useless in answering the question, how does your organization deliver value?

An operating model depicts core capabilities necessary to deliver value and how they are linked to each other. It enables a shared story of how an organization works together across functions and with its partners to deliver value.

Capabilities are the building blocks of an operating model. Every capability is comprised of three elements: people, process, and technology. A capability integrates people aligned to accomplish a structured set of activities enabled by technology to produce a desired outcome. In plain speak a capability is simply the power to do something.

For example, you might have the capability or power to make a mean western omelet. You possess the skill (people) thanks to hands-on training from mom, a recipe (process) handed down for generations, and a great cook-top range, nonstick pan, and spatula (technology). Of course, making a great western omelet for your family at home doesn't mean your capability can scale to making omelets for hundreds at a busy breakfast restaurant. A significant element of capability thinking and planning is not only how to integrate people, process, and technology for a single capability but to understand what it takes to scale each capability and how they all link together to form a winning operating model. A successful breakfast restaurant must do more than have a capability to make a great omelet. Its operating model integrates multiple capabilities including creating demand to eat at the restaurant, making sure fresh ingredients are on hand in the right quantities, offering friendly table service, attracting and retaining a motivated group of skilled employees, and managing the books, just to name a few. The restaurant only succeeds if each capability performs at a high level and all of the capabilities are integrated to delight the customer.

Having a great concept to create value isn't enough. It is equally important to be able to deliver on your value proposition to every customer every day.

Try taking your organization chart and converting it into a picture of your current operating model. Think about your operating model as a network of capabilities. Start by just listing your company's capabilities. It will force you to think about what your organization actually has the power to do. Then sort them based on their relative importance to delivering customer value. Which capabilities are core to delivering on your value proposition and which ones play only a supporting role? For instance, the capability to introduce a steady stream of new products and services may be core to value delivery, while the capability to ensure a steady supply of paper clips on every employee's desk is certainly secondary (nothing against paper clips or those responsible for procuring office supplies).

Core Capabilities	Key Enabling Capabilities	Supporting Capabilities
Example:Introducing a steady stream of new products and services	Example: Making great resource allocation decisions across product and service portfolio	Example: Ensuring communication infrastructure is in place and functioning
?	?	?
?	?	?

FIGURE 2.3 Capability Framework

It is helpful to sort capabilities into three categories (see Figure 2.3).

Which capabilities are most critical to how your company delivers value? For a pharmaceutical company it may be the capability to discover new compounds to treat cancer. For a department store chain it may be a logistics capability to stock each store with the hottest fashions. For an online retailer it may be a capability to offer amazing customer service. For a financial service company it may be the capability to develop the next great investment product. For every company there is a short list of capabilities that matter most to deliver value to its customers.

Once you have a good list of core capabilities and key enablers the next step in developing your business model story is to create an operating model picture that describes how core capabilities relate to each other and must be integrated to deliver customer value.

The project I led with the pharmaceutical company G.D. Searle back in 1995 provides a good example of going beyond organization charts to develop an operating model to describe how an organization delivers customer value. It also brings back interesting memories for me, having worked broadly throughout the pharmaceutical industry, comprised at the time of many midsized companies like Searle. Most of them (including Searle) no longer exist today, having been swallowed up by the massive industry consolidation that has occurred in the pharmaceutical industry over the last 15 years. When I worked with Searle in the 1990s they were a wholly owned subsidiary of the agricultural company Monsanto. In 2000

Searle merged with another midsized pharmaceutical company, Pharmacia, which had already merged with Upjohn, and ultimately all three were merged in to the current pharmaceutical giant Pfizer. Today's pharmaceutical industry screams for business model innovation, which is a topic we will come back to in later chapters, but for now, back to the Searle project example.

The new Searle CEO, Richard De Schutter, asked us to work with his leadership team to create a new operating model or way of working that better aligned functional activities to deliver customer value and improve the company's operating performance. The main challenge faced by Searle, and one faced by many of the companies I worked with and observed over the years, was deep functional silos that did not work effectively together. It looked good on an organization chart but did not operate in a coordinated way to deliver customer value and optimize organizational performance. Marketing did not work well with sales. Research did not work well with development. The research and development organization was not aligned with commercial parts of the organization. Manufacturing and distribution was not well-integrated with the commercial and R&D functions. And the international division was run completely separate from the U.S. operation, with little global coordination. Sound familiar?

It was immediately obvious that we needed a way to get senior executives talking about a shared operating vision that broke down functional silos and organization chart boundaries. If we were going to help the company's leaders and the people who worked for them in their respective parts of the organization to work together to deliver customer value in a new way, we needed a new story they could relate to and share about how the organization did its work. We needed a picture that enabled everyone in the organization to see how they each fit into the value delivery puzzle and how they related to each other regardless of where they lived in the organization chart.

We started by forming a design team comprised of representatives from each of the key functional areas across the company. We chose leaders who were respected within their functions and who had bought into the idea that the current way the organization worked needed to be changed. They knew that while each of their functions may have been doing good work, measured by their own functional yardsticks, they were not working well together and the overall organization was underperforming as a result.

We asked each of the members of our design team to begin doodling pictures of how they thought the organization was operating to deliver customer value. Back of the envelope and napkin doodles are a good place to start. They began to move from the organization chart to simple pictures that reflected how the existing functions related to each other. They created a picture of their "as is" operating model (see Figure 2.4).

From this most basic picture executives were able to start talking about how they operated and where the overlap was between their functional silos. We spent days focused on each of the overlaps mapping out key areas and integration points where collaboration was critical between functions. We asked executives to think of each area not as a box on an organization chart but as a capability that was necessary to deliver customer value. Each capability was

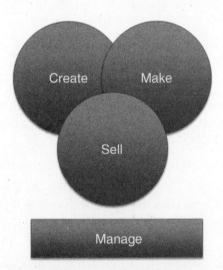

FIGURE 2.4 "As Is" Operating Model Picture

critically dependent on the other and it quickly became clear that a capability did not mean a function or a department because each capability required input, support, and work from multiple functions across the organization.

The Searle project team quickly realized their simple operating model picture mapped closely to the current organization chart but did not tell the story of how they wanted to operate going forward. It reflected their "as is" operating model but didn't clearly explain their core strategy to create customer value by focusing within four key disease or therapeutic areas: cardiovascular, insomnia, cancer, and arthritis. The team began to redraw their operating model picture (see Figure 2.5).

In this operating model picture the team explored fully integrated business units, each with their own capabilities to discover, develop, manufacture, distribute, market, and sell products within

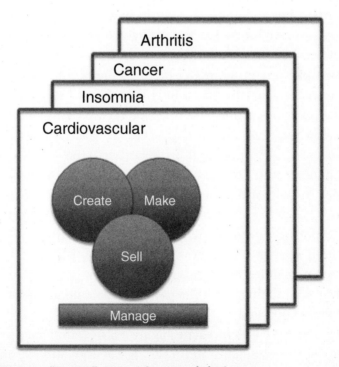

FIGURE 2.5 "To Be" Operating Model Picture

respective therapeutic areas or product groupings. The difference between the two operating visions was dramatic and the simple pictures provided a powerful way for executives to discuss and ultimately align around a shared story of how they wanted to operate to deliver customer value and improve organizational performance. A simple operating model picture provides a framework to ask how everyday business events and activities will be conducted and managed in any operating model vision and provides a way to compare and contrast alternative operating models.

Once we had operating model pictures to share with the broader organization we could begin to test how it would work and if it made sense by stressing each operating vision with real business events and situations. We set up business event walkthroughs with representatives from across multiple functions and management levels throughout the company. We shared the operating model pictures, practicing our stories about how the company currently worked and how it might be able to work better going forward. Business event walkthroughs were enlightening, enabling the design team to iterate toward a workable new operating vision for Searle.

From these operating model pictures the Searle team began to translate each capability into a fully fleshed-out listing of core and enabling processes, skills, and roles for each process, and enabling technology required for each process. Ultimately Searle implemented a new operating model, a hybrid between the two pictures creating therapeutic area business units but keeping some of the capabilities outside of the business units managed central to supply services to each business unit. The end result was an entirely new way of working within Searle and better alignment of functions to the overall strategic mission of the company. The company was much better at allocating resources and aligning activities across the organization to deliver customer value and company performance significantly improved.

Operating model pictures are highly organization-specific. They can have a powerful effect and meaning for those directly involved and seem trivial to outside observers. Don't underestimate the importance of creating a shared operating vision, serving to align key stakeholders and to focus activities and resources. A shared operating model picture enables the entire organization to see how they are expected to contribute to delivering customer value. It also sends a clear signal to the organization on how departments and functions are expected to collaborate with a shared purpose for value delivery. Which capabilities are most important to your organization to deliver value to your customers? What is the shared operating vision that describes how capabilities are networked to deliver value in your company? What does an operating model picture look like for your company?

How Does Your Organization Capture Value?

Most think a business model is only about how an organization makes money. It isn't. A business model story has all three elements, including how a company creates, delivers, and captures value. Nonetheless, a sustainable financial model is a key element of any successful business model. A business model story describes who pays and how much for value delivered. It outlines a profit formula for the business based on the required operating cost structure in relation to revenue as well as the capital requirements to finance both fixed assets and working capital to support ongoing operations and growth.

The first step in articulating a financial model is describing a company's revenue sources. Who pays? Seems like such a straightforward question. It isn't always. Often the person or intermediary who pays the bill creating revenue isn't the value recipient at all. Most patients don't pay directly for their own health care. Many students don't pay their own college tuition bill. As consumers, there are often many intermediaries between us and the company or organization actually responsible for value creation. When we buy clothing or food from the local boutique or supermarket, revenue is produced supporting the business model of the retailer. When the retailer replenishes its inventory it produces revenue supporting the business model of a local distributor. And when the distributor replenishes its inventory or agrees to stock the merchandise from the fashion designer or farmer, it produces revenue to support their respective business models. Each player in this example has a discreet business model story of how they create, deliver, and capture value.

It isn't unusual for the actual end-user, or the person for whom value is being created, to not be the one who actually pays the bill. Every business model clearly identifies who pays the bill and how revenue is generated. It is also important to identify other players that are critical to delivering value to the actual end-user and who may influence the actual purchase decision.

Another important aspect of articulating how a business model captures value is not just identifying where revenue comes from but also to specify what the customer is paying for. Is revenue created in your business model by selling a product, a service, or by bundling both? Does the customer pay you for each unit consumed or for all they can consume within a certain time? Examples include: a separate price for each ride in the amusement park or a single price admission to ride all the rides, an à la carte menu at a restaurant or a prix fixe chef's special, a price per movie rented or a monthly fee for unlimited movie usage. Is revenue a function of how much time it takes to deliver a service or based on delivering a specified outcome? For example, a lawyer charging by the hour or a fixed fee to deliver an estate plan, a builder charging by the day or agreeing to build a house for a flat fee, a health care company getting paid by procedure, or by caring for a population for a set fee.

Pricing also plays an important role in determining how a business model captures value. Pricing is the least understood and most poorly implemented element of the marketing mix. Whenever you see an overreliance on discounts and incentives to boost sales it's a red flag. Leading with price is a sure sign of an undifferentiated product or service. Far too many marketing and sales organizations overuse incentives and discounts. That's because it's easier to sell at a lower price than work to convince customers of the value inherent in a higher price. It's also human nature to sell at a lower price rather than accept the risk of losing a sale. The problem is that discounting behavior sends a message to consumers that the offering isn't worth the asking price. Inevitably, customers will simply wait for a better deal. Selling on price is like a drug addiction. Once discounting behavior creeps into an organization it's difficult to control the habit.

I learned this lesson early in my career while working at Eli Lilly & Co. in a corporate pricing job. I was responsible for bringing discount requests from a large field sales organization directly to the president of the company. He reviewed every request no matter how small and I wondered why. Clearly discounting behavior was unwelcome in the sales organization. The organization learned that differentiating product value by holding the price line and accepting manageable risk was the only winning strategy. The process also provided a great window to assess field management talent for future promotions. As often as I tried to explain this to field sales managers, they still spun incredible stories about how their business was at risk and if they couldn't offer a discount, "all would be lost."

I observed the same discounting behavior at many companies across multiple industries during my years as a strategy consultant. Once a discounting addiction takes hold in an organization only a significant rehabilitation effort, usually including personnel changes, can turn a downward pricing spiral around. Market pricing strategies are also being turned on their head by upstart business model innovators who have developed digital offerings they can offer for significantly less or even for free to your customers, creating enormous pressure on existing business models. This is one of the biggest reasons business model innovation has become a strategic imperative for all leaders. What role does pricing play in your current business model? How much are discounting and special pricing practices affecting the revenue produced by your business model?

The second half of the profit formula after identifying revenue sources is, of course, the operating cost side of the equation. How much does it cost to deliver value? What are the elements of the cost structure of your business model and how do they support value delivery? Which costs are variable and directly tied to unit sales and revenue levels? Which costs are fixed representing required infrastructure and assets to support the business model? How heavily is your business model dependent on fixed costs? How are financial resources allocated across your business model? Are you able to associate costs with those core capabilities you identified most critical to deliver customer value? Is there revenue left over after operating costs are covered to reinvest in the business model and to scale it to support growth? What are the profit and growth expectations from your current business model?

Cost structure, infrastructure requirements, and financing models play an important role in any business model. They represent an architecture that provides financial fuel to the business model to enable ongoing value creation and delivery. They play a lead role in business decision making and, as we will explore in later chapters, are often a significant obstacle to business model innovation.

Putting the Entire Business Model Story Together

A great business model story relates all three of the core business model elements.

First, answer the three core questions posed in this chapter:

How does your company create value?
How does your company deliver value?
How does your company capture value?

It is now time to stitch your answers together into a cohesive business model story. The best tool I have found to map your current business model and to frame a compelling story is the Business Model Canvas. This easy to use business model mapping tool was originally published in *Business Model Generation* by Alexander Osterwalder and is now also available as an iPad app. I highly recommend both to anyone interested in business models.

Before you can start exploring business model innovation it is important to understand the core elements of a business model and to be able to map your current business model. Use the Business Model Canvas to outline the elements of your current business model and shape a story to describe the way your company creates, delivers, and captures value (see Figure 2.6).

Now that we have covered Business Model 101 we can move on to the good stuff. How do you transform your business model and why is it imperative that all leaders learn how to do R&D for new business models the same way they do today for new products and technologies?

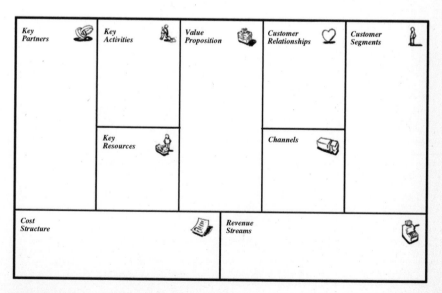

FIGURE 2.6 Business Model Canvas

3 Why Organizations Fail at Business Model Innovation

rganizations fail at business model innovation because they are so busy pedaling the bicycle of their current business models they leave no time, attention, or resources to design, prototype, and test new ones. Far too much of our innovation focus today is on new products and services delivered through today's business models and on driving efficiencies into the current models. These are important activities, but not sufficient in a twenty-first century networked world where business models don't last as long as they used to.

While it's always necessary and important to strengthen current business models, it isn't sufficient if you want to avoid being net-flixed. Leaders focus almost exclusively on improving their current business models at the expense of exploring new ones. The good news is that leaders have really embraced innovation as a strategy for growth. The bad news is innovation initiatives are all over the place, everyone is an innovator and everything is described as an innovation. When that happens no one is an innovator and nothing is an innovation. Most of the innovation efforts I have observed over the years, across industries and companies, are focused on improving the performance of the current business model. They are either an effort to source or develop new products and services to create new revenue within the current business model or an attempt to deploy new and improved capabilities within the current model to increase revenue or decrease costs. These are both important activities, but neither will prevent an organization from being netflixed by a disruptive business model.

Forgive me, but I can't resist using a consultant's two-by-two matrix to describe why most organizations fail at business model innovation (see Figure 3.1).

Most of the innovation efforts I have observed or supported as a road warrior consultant have been about either developing a better mousetrap or a better way to create, make, and sell today's mousetrap. Corporate innovation efforts are rarely focused beyond rhetoric on creating entirely new paradigms for controlling mice. Now

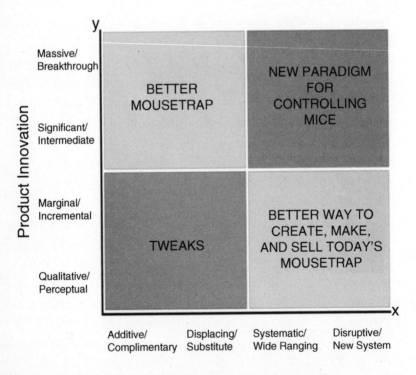

FIGURE 3.1   Why Business Model Innovation Matters

before you start screaming, don't get me wrong, incremental improvements are important and must be captured. There are a gazillion consultants and great business books covering how to deliver incremental improvements to a business model. I am not implying that these efforts aren't necessary, just that they aren't sufficient to avoid being disrupted. This book focuses on how to get beyond incremental improvements to also include business model innovation in your innovation armamentarium.

Most organizations fail at business model innovation because of an overreliance on tweaks. It is not for lack of trying. Almost every company I visit has a crazy number of well-intentioned initiatives going on across the organization. I call this phenomenon "death by 1,000 initiatives." The initiatives are often redundant and rarely connected strategically. Every business unit, geography, and function each has a number of projects going on simultaneously, all intended to improve the performance of the current business model. Most set out initially to accomplish more than tweaks. Bold language at the outset of every project always includes lofty aspirations from senior executives challenging the project team to reach for transformational solutions and going beyond tweaks. But when senior executives leave and the real work begins, line management and risk adverse human behavior sets in. Most projects are designed to deliver tweaks or incremental improvement to either product portfolio or organization performance; they are constrained by the DNA and rules of the current business model.

On the vertical or y-axis of the matrix is product and service innovation. Improved performance by traveling up this dimension ranges from tweaks or minor enhancement of product and service features to more significant improvements or better mousetraps. New product and service development commands most of the typical organization's innovation attention and resources. It is the most straightforward way to sustain and improve the performance of an existing business model. Once a business model establishes its competitive market, go-to-market capabilities, and economics, the best source of profitable growth is to leverage the model with a steady flow of new products and services. Traditional product- and service-focused research and development is the first source of innovation for most organizations and the only source for many.

The challenge most companies face over time is that a product and service arms race with industry competitors all trying to best each other with a steady stream of product and service extensions and new features becomes increasingly difficult to sustain over time. The bigger a company gets the higher the expectation for new product and service development. Replacing revenue from aging products and services nearing the end of their life cycles and adding new revenue to support growth objectives becomes the singular focus of the organization. Companies become increasingly dependent on introducing homerun products and services with greater frequency in order to meet growth expectations. Over time, products and services that meet customer needs but with small initial market potential look less and less attractive and are discarded as viable opportunities. As Clay Christensen teaches us with his disruptive innovation theory, this leaves a big gap in the market for disrupters to fill. As companies move further upstream meeting the needs of their best customers at higher price points with more product and service features, disrupters are left alone to enter the market at the bottom with new products, services, and business models. And as Christensen also often reminds us, companies don't disrupt themselves. Focusing exclusively on product and service innovation isn't sustainable. Business model innovation must be part of every company's innovation agenda and platform.

On the horizontal or x-axis is capability innovation. Improved performance by traveling across this dimension ranges from tweaks or minor enhancement of existing capabilities to more significant capability improvements or better ways to create, make, and sell today's mousetraps. In most organizations capability innovation efforts are fragmented throughout the organization owned and driven by functional leaders. The efforts tend to be episodic and incremental. Initiatives to build cross-functional capabilities are incredibly painful and typically start out with bold objectives and end up achieving a fraction of the expected business results after enormous cost and distraction to the organization. If you have ever been part of an initiative to install new enterprise software with the promise of transformation in customer relationship management, supply chain, or enterprise financial management, you know exactly what I mean. Just thinking about it reminds me of my road warrior consulting days and all of the black and blue marks and scars! I don't mean to be so negative, but most of these initiatives set out to change the way an organization delivers value and ended up being a way to take costs out of the current business model. Keeping operating costs low is important, but by itself will not sustain a business model facing the threat of disruptive new business models.

Capability innovation in most organizations falls into the best practices trap. What are the practices among our competitors and how can we replicate the best ones? I am always amazed at how many executives think out-executing competition on core industry practices is a sustainable source of competitive advantage. It has also become fashionable to look for best practices among noncompetitors that can be replicated for competitive advantage. The problem is that when interesting practices are discovered they are assessed within the context of the current business model, not whether they could enable a new business model or way to create, deliver, and capture value. Company's innovation lenses need to expand beyond how to improve the efficiency of the current business model to how can existing capabilities be redeployed or new capabilities be deployed in new business model configurations to change the customer value equation.

Companies fail at business model innovation because their innovation lenses and practices never reach the upper right quadrant of the matrix to design, prototype, and test new paradigms for controlling mice.

10 Reasons Companies Fail at Business Model Innovation

1. CEOs Don't Really Want a New Business Model

The most obvious reason companies fail at business model innovation is because CEOs and their senior leadership teams don't want to explore new business models. They are content with the current one and want everyone in the organization focused on how to improve its performance. The clearest indication that an organization and its leaders aren't interested in business model innovation is when any discussion about emerging business models in the market or about potentially disruptive technology is viewed and treated solely as a competitive threat.

If leaders make it an explicit choice to go "all in" on the current business model, at least the direction to and expectations for the organization are clear. If business model innovation is off the table, innovation teams can focus on the mandate to help the organization develop better mousetraps and to deliver improved capabilities to create, make, sell, and manage them. If, on the other hand, it's an implicit choice to ignore business model innovation as a strategic option and the current business model is at risk of disruption, it's only a matter of time until bad things start to happen. With the half-life of any business model declining, ignoring options for business model innovation is a very risky choice for any leader and all organizations.

2. Business Model Innovation Will Be the Next CEO's Problem

Let the next guy or gal handle it. The prevailing industry business model has been in place since before I was in charge and it will still be in place after I leave. I don't want to be known as the CEO who precipitated the end of a successful business model. There may very well be disruptive models and technologies on the horizon but we can beat them back, get laws passed to slow them down, and treat them as minor nuisances and the niche players they will always be. Sound familiar? Today's CEOs have never had to change their business models. Neither have their peers. They didn't teach business model innovation in business school. It should be no surprise that CEOs aren't in a hurry to establish a company capability for business model innovation. I don't think they have bought into the idea that the half-life of any business model is declining. They view what Netflix did to Blockbuster as an exception and not the rule. It isn't going to happen to us—until it does.

While it may be true that today's CEOs have never had to change their business models, the CEO of tomorrow is likely to have to change their business models several times over the course of his or her career. As the pace of disruptive technology diffusion quickens, trying to outlast the current business model curve is a risky strategy. Leaving the challenge to the next CEO is not such a good idea.

3. Product Is King—Nothing Else Matters

Companies that consider themselves product-centric typically create deep product cultures reinforcing the notion throughout the organization that product is king. Everything about the business model centers on managing a product portfolio. Product-centric business models have a blind spot when it comes to the role services play in their value propositions. Services are considered a value-add. The product comes first and then services add value to the proposition. The customer often doesn't see it that way. The customer has a job to do and assesses any business model's value proposition as a bundle of product and service.

Value-add is like the toy a child finds inside of their cereal box. The toy is only a temporary part of the product's value proposition. I don't know about your children, but mine always selected the cereal box from the grocery store shelf based on what toy was inside it. When they went to the grocery store the next time, if there was a better toy inside another cereal brand they selected it. They had no loyalty to one cereal brand. The toy is a value-add and not a sustainable part of the core value proposition.

Today the lines are blurring between product and service. Business models that are exclusively focused on products are vulnerable to being disrupted by models that blend both product and service to significantly change the value proposition. Not as a value-add to the product, but as a transformational change to the value proposition and business model. Think iPod. Apple didn't bring the first MP3 player to the market. It changed the way we experienced music by delivering on a value proposition that bundled product and service. iTunes was not a value-add to the iPod—it was part of the core value proposition. Apple created a new business model around the bundle. Apple didn't think of itself as a product-centric company. If it did it would have viewed the other MP3 manufacturers as the competition. The competition wasn't a product manufacturer at all; it was Tower Records and other music retailers where we went to buy record albums and CDs. Apple changed the value proposition and disrupted an entire industry, leaving product-centric MP3 manufacturers in the dust.

Industrial-era thinking and NAICS industry codes force companies into characterizing their business models as being either product- or service-focused. This is a false choice. We are still talking about manufacturing as if it's an industry sector rather than a business capability. Making a product doesn't define the market a company is creating or competing within. Describing a business as a manufacturer immediately constrains the business model and business model innovation opportunities. Apple manufactures great products, but it isn't just a manufacturing company. Business model innovation is about starting with the job that a customer is trying to do and then shaping a value proposition and delivery model to help the customer get the job done. Sometimes a proud product heritage can get in the way.

4. Information Technology Is Only about Keeping the Trains Moving and Lowering Costs

I'm from IT and I am here to help you! Many companies fail at business model innovation because the majority of information technology department resources and activities end up being allocated to supporting legacy systems. Most of the effort goes to keeping current IT systems running and patching holes when they occur. Current information systems must be kept functioning with downtime at an absolute minimum. Nothing gets an IT executive in deeper trouble than an operating disruption in a mission critical process due to an IT system going down. Legacy systems take priority and over time grow to consume most of the IT capacity within an organization.

If there is any IT staff capacity or resource remaining within the department's budget for new development, initiatives are typically justified through operating cost reductions. Information technology is primarily used to sustain and to make incremental efficiency improvements to the current business model. The first question typically asked to justify new IT development work is, how long will it take to recover the cost of the new system through a reduction in operating costs? The second question asked is, how disruptive will it be to current operations to install the new systems and to train staff to use it? Transitions involving any decline in current operating performance, even if temporary, are heavily frowned upon. Maybe we don't need to do that new system development work this year. Rarely did I hear the question, can this information system enable an entirely new business model and a way to deliver value to our customers?

The prevalence of enterprise systems that cut across functional units is a big barrier to business model innovation. Once enterprise systems are in place any change anywhere within the organization affects every other function, making it extremely difficult to develop new functional capabilities let alone consider an entirely new business model. Every change in the current business model affects every other component of the model. Therefore, to change any of it requires that the entire enterprise change, thus making the safest course of action to change none of it. Enterprise systems are great to increase the efficiency of the current business model, but end up being straitjackets constraining business model innovation.

5. Cannibalization Is off the Table

The last thing we want to do is risk any of our current business. It's hard enough being at war with the competition in a battle for market share; why would we want to compete against ourselves? We need new products and services that will add revenue on top of our current sales, not take away from our current base of business. Don't do anything that puts our current customer base at risk. These and many sentiments like them are frequently heard from line executives if any new product, service, or business model idea is introduced that may cannibalize current business. Sometimes the sentiment is expressed explicitly but more often it is implicit in management decision-making and behavior. It is human nature to fight to keep what you already have. Risking what you already have for the possibility of something better is not the normal tendency for people or organizations.

Cannibalization isn't just about new products replacing existing products, but also applies to new business models replacing current ones. Blockbuster didn't see the DVD-by-mail business model as an opportunity to open up entirely new customer market segments; it saw it initially as a distracting niche and later as a competitive threat. By the time it decided to play in the market created by Netflix, it was too late and they were only playing catch up. When executives look at a new business model opportunity they tend to see it through the lens of the current business model and view it as cannibalizing the current way the organization creates, delivers, and captures value. Organizations fail at business model innovation because they blindly take cannibalization off the table even if the new business model has significant upside potential.

6. Nowhere Near Enough Connecting with Unusual Suspects

Senior executives need to get out more. They spend far too much time in the office and not nearly enough time out in the market. When they do get out they tend to meet with the usual suspects, the same people they always meet with. The topics are always the same and the discussions are all too predictable. How can leaders expect to learn anything new if they don't mingle with unusual suspects, people with different perspectives and experiences than their own? Organizations fail at business model innovation because they spend too much time inside the echo chambers within their own companies and industries. The same solutions and practices are shopped around over and over. Time spent out of the office at industry trade meetings is more about showing up so competitors won't speculate on your absence and making sure competitors aren't getting an upper hand than about looking for new practices and potential new business models that can change the customer value equation.

Business model innovation is often about combining and recombining capabilities in new ways. Exposure to more ideas from unusual suspects and places often creates the spark needed for a new business model concept. Catalyzing business model innovation requires fresh and new perspectives, the kind of perspectives that can't be found by insulating leaders within the confines of the organization and industry. Business model innovation is more about next practices than best practices. Next practices are far more likely to be informed by unusual suspects and found in the gray areas between silos, sectors, and disciplines.

7. Line Executives Hold Your Pay Card

Who wants to volunteer to work on an exciting project to explore potential new business models for our organization? It's an exciting opportunity to be part of helping us to create our future. It will be a temporary assignment and then you will return to your functional home within the organization. And oh, by the way, your performance and salary review will still be conducted by your current boss. Don't worry because your regular job will still be waiting for you when you finish this special project. No wonder most change ends up being incremental no matter how lofty the objectives are at the outset of an innovation project. Line executives who hold project team member pay cards inevitably exert subtle and not-so-subtle pressure to focus on things that will help their respective business units or functions. And they lean against anything that is distracting or potentially disruptive to their organizational units.

Line executives are tasked with making sure the current business model works well and to improve its performance. When innovation departments are accountable to line management it should come as no surprise to anyone that project priorities will focus on ways to support and improve the current business model. There's nothing wrong with that but don't expect business model innovation to be in the project mix. Business model innovation will not make the short list of things for line executives to focus on. They will inevitably work to steer resources and organizational focus toward things that will help the current business model. How excited is anyone likely to be to work on a new disruptive business model if their career is in the hands of a boss who is vested in the current business model?

8. Great Idea, What's the ROI?

There's no easier way to prevent or lean against business model innovation than to assess initiatives to design, prototype and test potential new models using the same economics and financial metrics as projects to improve the performance of the current business model. One size does not fit all innovation projects when it comes to resourcing business model innovation projects and assessing their financial impact. The finance tools used to manage a product or capability development portfolio are a function of the economics of the current business model. Inputs include the expected impact on revenues, costs, margins, and invested assets. Financial metrics utilized to assess alternative projects to improve the current business model reflect the cost structure and required returns to sustain and grow in the context of today's model. New business models are likely to have very different economics and must be assessed in that context. Most new business models will be dismissed out of hand if judged by the economics and constrained by the ROI requirements of the current model.

Different economics doesn't mean unfavorable economics. By burdening the assessment of a new business model with expected returns that must support the overhead and cost structure of the current model organizations set up a self-fulfilling prophecy preventing business model innovation. The only innovation projects that make financial sense are those that add incremental value to the current business model. Organizations fail at business model innovation because they apply the wrong financial lens in assessing the attractiveness and feasibility of new business models. The economics of Netflix look terrible when measured by return per square feet of retail space and return on value of long-term lease holdings.

9. They Shoot Business Model Innovators, Don't They?

Organizations fail at business model innovation because they shoot their renegades. If they don't shoot them they wear them down until they leave. Business model innovators go against the corporate grain. They see entirely new ways to create, deliver, and capture value. If those that are tasked with sustaining and growing today's business models are allowed to reject those with the perspective and insight to help design the next one, business model innovation efforts will fail. They will fail if the antigens built up in the organization prevent business model innovators from thriving. Organizations must learn to celebrate and support people within the organization who are willing to challenge the status quo, to bring totally different perspectives on delivering value to the table, and are willing to take experimental risks to explore new models.

Applying the same performance management and promotion systems to business model innovators as those working to add value to the current business model will not work. Renegades work and are motivated differently.

It is easy to find the renegades and business model innovators within every organization. It is also easy to see if they are enabled or disabled. Organizations fail because they don't establish the conditions and platforms for business model innovation to happen. They fail because they don't differentiate between innovation efforts to produce better mousetraps and better ways to create, make, and sell today's mousetraps from efforts to develop entirely new paradigms for controlling mice. Business model innovation is different than product and capability innovation and requires unique platforms, tools, and skills. The characteristics of a business model innovator are different too. They must be welcomed into the organization and supported from the corner office. Line management will eat business model innovators alive if they don't have cover from the top. It doesn't take long to listen to an organization's stories and know if it shoots its business model innovators.

10. You Want to Experiment in the Real World; Are You Crazy?

Organizations fail at business model innovation because ideas never make it from the whiteboard into the real world. It's easy to doodle a new business model concept on a whiteboard. It's easy for a consultant to put together a deck describing how a new business model might work. It's hard to know with any certainty if a new business model concept is viable in the market. New business models have to be prototyped and tested in the real world. They can't be tested on paper. They can't be tested in a conference room. Business models require experimentation. This is what entrepreneurs do. They try stuff to see if it works. Intrapreneurs are no different. They try out multiple business models until they find one that works and can scale. They don't rely on fancy plans, financial analysis, or reports to start because they don't know if a model will work. Business model experiments need to be both easy to start and to stop. Failing fast is a key requirement for successful business model innovation. To be successful at business model innovation, leaders are going to have to get comfortable with experimenting with new business models in the real world. Leaders will have to overcome their resistance to exploring new business models, even those that may be disruptive to the current one.

While there are many reasons organizations fail at business model innovation, it is time to stop admiring the problems and to start exploring the new strategic imperative for all leaders who want to stay relevant in a changing world. R&D for new business models is the new strategic imperative.

Connect, Inspire, Transform: 15 Business Model Innovation Principles

If you want to transform your business model I highly recommend you start by mapping your organization's genome. Understanding the basic genetic code or wiring of any organization is key to understanding what drives the behavior of both internal and external stakeholders. Intimate knowledge of your genome's chromosomal makeup is a prerequisite for alignment and making meaningful progress. It explains why employees, customers, and collaborators are attracted to an organization or why they aren't. Passion for an organization, community, or movement is coded at the genetic level. If you want to transform an organization forget process reengineering and think genetic reengineering. If you want to launch a new business model, make your genome transparent and accessible to anyone with a similar genetic make-up.

In this section of the book I offer fifteen business model innovation principles that will set the stage for creating your own business model innovation factory. These principles are based on our work at the Business Innovation Factory (BIF), where over the last eight years we have connected with thousands of like-minded innovation junkies and organizations and have observed a common pattern of characteristics that defines them at their core. We call it the BIF Genome and have found it very helpful in working with organizations and communities that want to establish a business model innovation factory. These principles describe the conditions necessary to enable business model innovation. They can help you assess if you, your organization, or your community has the genetic wiring to transform the way value is created, delivered, and captured. We believe that innovators are wired differently. The BIF Genome was developed to help identify 15 fundamental principles that define the collective DNA of business model innovators.

These 15 business model innovation principles are described over the three chapters of this section organized around the business model innovation mantra: Connect. Inspire. Transform.

Connect: Business Model Innovation Is a Team Sport

1. Catalyze something bigger than yourself.
2. Enable random collisions of unusual suspects.
3. Collaborative innovation is the mantra.
4. Build purposeful networks.
5. Together, we can design our future.

Inspire: We Do What We Are Passionate About

6. Stories can change the world.
7. Make systems-level thinking sexy.
8. Transformation is itself a creative act.
9. Passion rules—exceed your own expectations.
10. Be inspiration accelerators.

Transform: Incremental Change Isn't Working

11. Tweaks won't do it.
12. Experiment all the time.
13. Get off the whiteboard and into the real world.
14. It's a user center world—design for it.
15. A decade is a terrible thing to waste.

As you read these principles in the next three chapters ask yourself, does your organization share a similar genetic makeup? Do these principles resonate with you?

4 Connect: Business Model Innovation Is a Team Sport

Innovation is a team sport that requires collaboration, learning, and experimentation across silos, industry sectors, and disciplines. No one person, function, or organization has all the answers.

Principle 1. Catalyze Something Bigger Than Yourself

Business model innovation starts by realizing you are contributing to a movement that is bigger than you. It's global, self-organizing, and transformative. Lead by letting go. The first and most important step in the business model innovation process requires a change in perspective for both you and your organization. Looking through the lens of your current business model will most likely result in incremental changes at best. Business model innovation requires a different perspective. It requires a different set of lenses to examine new opportunities. It starts by realizing transformational opportunities are bigger than you and your organization. Business model innovation must be treated like an epoch journey with all the wide-eyed enthusiasm of a young child exploring new territory for the first time.

Business model innovation must be a strategic objective or it won't happen. One of my biggest pet peeves is setting strategy one tactic at a time. It drives me crazy to be surrounded by people and organizations that think if they just work hard enough and do more things that a strategic direction and destination will emerge. It seems that most of the world works this way. It is terribly inefficient. How many people and organizations do you know that pedal the bicycle like crazy but never seem to arrive anywhere? They just keep pedaling harder, hoping that something will eventually stick. It is exhausting watching them. Why not establish business model innovation as a strategic objective, a specific destination, and work hard on those things that help you get there? It seems so simple. Setting a strategic direction provides a way to know which tactics are aligned and contribute to reaching the destination. The destination may change along the way, requiring different tactics, and that is okay, but not having a destination at all is a ticket to nowhere.

When John F. Kennedy said, "We choose to go to the moon" in 1961, Americans rallied around the destination. We believed it was possible, and the goal of setting foot on the moon rallied a country to advance its global science and technology leadership. It was cool to study math and science and clear that innovation was the economic engine that would drive American prosperity. When Neil Armstrong set foot on the moon eight years later and said, "That's one small step for man, one giant leap for mankind," we celebrated his achievement as if it was our own and knew at that moment that anything was possible. We have been trying to get that feeling back ever since. Today, we have no clear destination, in space or on earth.

I am still trying to process President Obama's plan to cancel NASA's Constellation program for manned space flight back to the moon. Okay, I thought, maybe he has a bolder, more imaginative space destination in mind or a better way to get back to the moon.

It turns out that the announced strategy identifies no new destination at all and has been called a "flexible path" focusing on enabling technologies. The destination will be determined later. Please say it isn't so. It is impossible to be inspired without a destination and it is terribly inefficient to develop enabling technologies without an end in mind. It is enough to make you scream. All I can think of is the character Ralph Kramden in the television program *The Honeymooners* getting angry and red in the face, proclaiming, "To the moon, Alice!"

When setting out on a business model innovation journey it is impossible to know what a new business model will ultimately look like and how it will work. What is important is to establish a clear strategic objective to explore new business models, even those that may be disruptive to the current one. A bold business model innovation objective should inspire like a moon landing. By making the strategic objective clear it will send a strong message to everyone in the organization and provide a basis to align resources and activities necessary to enable business model innovation. You can't get there one tactic at a time, hoping it will add up to a bold new business model.

Business model innovation is also an epoch journey and requires daring to be great. Keith Yamashita, chairman of SYPartners and one of the most thoughtful and influential strategy consultants I know, asked the question that still haunts and compels me at one of BIF's annual Collaborative Innovation Summits (which brings together innovation junkies from around the world to share personal transformation stories). Keith asked the question, is it worth daring to be great? No consulting buzzwords, no ambiguity, just a simple question for all of us to ponder. Implied within Keith's question is the presumption we can all be great. We just have to dare to do it. Greatness isn't something conferred or willed by others. It isn't an entitlement or an inheritance. Greatness is innate and waiting for us to dare to achieve it. Keith rightly suggests greatness isn't a deficit that you have to fill. We unlearn greatness. We permit "the system" to suppress greatness. We start to believe what other people say about us as true. Kids don't start out that way. Kids are innately and wonderfully curious about the world around them until, sadly, society wears the enthusiasm and opportunity for greatness down. All kids start great.

I'm reminded of Michelangelo saying, "every block of stone has a statue inside and it is the task of the sculptor to discover it." The same is true for people and organizations. Each is born with an incredible sculpture inside. We all have greatness within us and it's our opportunity and responsibility to discover it. We must be our own sculptors and not wait or depend on being sculpted by others. If we're waiting for permission to be great we will be waiting a very long time. Compelling sculptures are born of self-exploration and personal passion. Greatness comes from within. It's not up to parents, teachers, friends, and bosses to do the sculpting but to encourage us, create the conditions, and provide the tools for self-sculpting.

Greatness comes from within and starts with the lighting of a fire. So back to Keith Yamashita's question: Is it worth daring to be great? Only you can answer the question for yourself and your organization. For this blessed and inspired innovation junkie my answer is, I don't think I could live with myself if I didn't dare to at least try.

If you don't think business model innovation is about catalyzing something bigger than yourself, just think about the self-organized quest for freedom in Egypt. It's hard to not be moved by the *cri de coeur* (cry of the heart) of the Egyptian people—a cry for freedom so loud the borders of Egypt couldn't contain it. I don't think I'm being hyperbolic in saying we are witness to the rise of a new world order. An era defined by entrenched public and private sector institutions is giving way, right before our eyes, to a new era defined by self-organization. Learning how to proactively transform your current business model is imperative before customers self-organize to disrupt it without you. While we have sensed the trend for awhile, the clarity and immediacy of the tangible quest for freedom in Cairo's Tahrir (Liberation) Square is riveting and marks a global inflection point. There is no turning back. Not in Egypt and not anywhere in the world. Self-organized purposeful networks enabled by social media will not be stopped. Fasten your seat belts.

Clay Shirky had it right when he warned us in his book, *Here Comes Everybody*. An era defined by self-organization is an equal opportunity disrupter. No institution will be unaffected. Any government not reflecting the will of the people isn't sustainable. Equally unsustainable are education systems not reflecting the will of the student, health care systems not reflecting the will of the patient, corporations not reflecting the will of the consumer, and economies not reflecting the will of the entrepreneur.

Institutions are designed for stability. They are designed to protect the status quo. They are designed to resist change and are allergic to even the hint of transformation. They are not designed to reflect the will of citizens, consumers, students, patients, and entrepreneurs. Your customers are now capable of self-organizing into purposeful networks that can bring about real transformation. Customers are just figuring out how to use their new network power and they don't have to wait for institutions to lead the way. The shift of power away from institutions will be messy. Entrenched institutions will not go quietly into the night. Transformations begun will inevitably have unintended consequences and we will all have to learn as we go, but there is no turning back. It isn't transformation that is impossible, it is sustaining the status quo that is impossible. Creating a business model innovation factory to stay out in front of or at least keep up with these societal changes is imperative.

Watching the events unfold in Egypt and around the world has been mesmerizing. It's too soon to know the outcomes and there are many scary implications and scenarios that could be unleashed by these self-organized uprisings. Regardless of the outcomes, when freedom is the underlying motivation, transformation is inevitable and its pace is quickening. When a butterfly flapped its wings in Tunisia it didn't take long for the ripple effect to show up in Egypt. I think the ripple is just getting started and it will impact your current business model in ways you can't even imagine today. Business model innovation is about catalyzing something bigger than yourself and your organization.

Principle 2. Enable Random Collisions of Unusual Suspects

Collaborators are everywhere. You will find them in the gray areas between silos. Just look up from your current business model. Seek out difference and gather often across boundaries, disciplines, and sectors. Be open and be curious. Beware of random collisions with unusual suspects. Unless, of course, if you want to learn something new. In that case seek out innovators from across every imaginable silo and listen, really listen, to their stories. New ideas, perspectives, and the big value-creating opportunities are in the gray areas between the unusual suspects. It seems so obvious and yet we spend most of our time with the usual suspects in our respective silos. We need to get out of our silos more.

It is human nature to surround ourselves with people who are exactly like us. We connect and spend time with people who share a common worldview, look the same, enjoy the same activities, and speak the same language. We join clubs to be with others like us. The club most worth belonging to is the nonclub club. The most valuable tribe is a tribe of unusual suspects who can challenge your worldview, expose you to new ideas, and teach you something new. A tribe of unusual suspects can change the world if it is connected in purposeful ways.

It is easy to see the potential from enabling random collisions of unusual suspects. Just check out any social media platform. Social media is a hotspot for random collisions. You don't need to hang out in these virtual places long to know they are populated with very unusual suspects. Interstitial spaces are ubiquitous and magic happens every day. We can bring this magic into our organizations, meetings, and gatherings. We just have to resist the normal tendency to hang out with the usual suspects. Most of the conferences and meetings we go to are teeming with usual suspects who love to get together to admire the problem. We sure do love to admire problems. Solution discussions are narrow and tend to shop around old solutions that have been discussed forever. If you want new ideas, approaches, and solutions go to gatherings that you have absolutely no reason to attend other than you might learn something new or meet somebody with a different perspective and experience. Make it a personal goal to attend gatherings where you don't know the people or subject matter. Or better yet, go to gatherings that are designed to bring unusual suspects together and to enable random collisions.

The goal is to get better faster. If you want to get better faster, hang out in interstitial spaces. Don't just dip your toes into interstitial spaces but jump in with all the passion you can ignite. Magic happens in the interstitial space between us. I saw the value of random collisions of unusual suspects when I spent six years working in state government in Rhode Island as an "accidental bureaucrat." I had a front row seat to observe the silos in action. As the smallest state in the United States, Rhode Island is a fascinating place for an innovation junkie to observe the way silos work. I could literally see the entire movie from my office. Everyone knows everyone else in the state. There are at most only two degrees of separation between any two people in Rhode Island. Every week went something like this: On Monday I met with the health care crowd, on Tuesday it was the education crowd, on Wednesday the energy crowd, and so on, you get the idea. This cycle repeated over and over again. Each crowd was comprised of the usual suspects, well-intentioned people rehashing the same discussion incessantly. The scene is right out of the movie *Groundhog Day*. Most of the participants were there to represent institutional perspectives and to protect their respective interests. In each crowd there are always a few innovators that want to change the conversation but they make little progress. At the end of each week I always came away with the same conclusion. If only we could take the innovators from across each of the silos and bring them together to enable more random collisions.

Maybe we could change the conversation if we connect more unusual suspects in purposeful ways. Maybe then we can make progress on transforming business models and social systems. Business model innovation takes cross-silo collaboration and breaking down the boundaries between industries, sectors, and disciplines. In constant heads-down mode, business model innovation isn't possible. Transformative business models are only possible if organizations learn how to experiment with new approaches that cut across protected silos. We need to think and act more horizontally.

We live and work in a networked world complete with mega bandwidth and social media platforms to help us collide with more unusual suspects if we just look up from our silos. These new connections can help us to design, prototype, and test new business models. It is time to try more stuff and take advantage of the disruptive innovation potential of all the technology we have within reach. We have more technology available to us than we know how to absorb. It isn't technology that gets in our way. It is our fault. Both humans and the organizations and silos we live in are stubbornly resistant to change. If we are receptive we can learn from innovators, especially the ones you will only find if you look in unusual places.

Business model innovators are all around us. They are taking advantage of today's technologies and creating new ways to deliver value. We can learn from them if we look up from our silos. Sometimes the most inspiring innovators are in places we would never have thought to look. Or perhaps we just don't notice them because we are so focused on our current business models and industries.

Meet the plumber and the police chief.

I first met Anthony Gemma while he was president of Gem Plumbing in Lincoln, Rhode Island. Together with his brothers, Anthony ran one of the most innovative businesses I have seen. I didn't expect it when I first visited the company. After all, how innovative can a plumbing supply company be? The answer is, very innovative.

Gem is on a mission to win the Baldrige National Quality Award. I believe they will achieve it. They have established a culture of excellence and innovation in every aspect of their regional business. They collect, analyze, and share data ranging from the location of every part—from the supplier to the service truck to the home—to how long a customer waits to talk live to the dispatcher on the phone. They benchmark themselves against the best. Not the best plumbing supply company, the best companies.

Gem's customer call and dispatch center would blow you away. It is like standing in NASA mission control. On 12-foot monitoring screens they have live feeds of real-time traffic conditions and satellite mapping of every service vehicle. If there is available capacity in the fleet, Gem places a customized radio ad to create tailored demand. They are so good at tracking traffic conditions they supply information to the Department of Transportation and local radio stations for traffic reports.

Gem Plumbing gets so many businesses coming in for tours and information about their innovation programs they set up the Gem Institute for Performance Excellence. Who would have thought to look at a regional plumbing supply company as an example of innovation best practices?

Next, meet Dean Esserman, who served as the chief of police in Providence, Rhode Island, from 2003 until 2011. When Chief Esserman arrived in Providence he found a city where the crime rates were high and a force that was troubled by corruption and distrusted by the community. People were afraid to travel downtown. What Esserman accomplished over eight years is a great story of business model innovation, and it delivered significant value to the citizens of Providence. You probably wouldn't have thought to look at the practices of a police chief to learn about business model innovation. Dean and other unusual suspects like him are often the best source of inspiring new business model ideas. You just have to look up from your silo.

In six years, Esserman transformed the Providence policing model from a centralized department where police were anonymous and came to the neighborhood after receiving a 911 call, to a decentralized department with neighborhood substations and district commanders who are accountable for crime in the local community. His philosophy is that when police get out of their cars and into the life of a neighborhood they become trusted allies.

I attended several of the chief's regular Tuesday morning command meetings, where a sophisticated crime tracking system displays crime statistics by district. Each commander is called upon to talk about crime activity in their district and what they are doing about it. The new business model is working, with double-digit declines in the overall Providence crime rate. Who would have thought to look at a police chief as an example of innovation best practices?

The plumber and the police chief are just two examples of the innovators among us. Examples are everywhere. We just have to look in the places that we would least expect to find them.

Principle 3. Collaborative Innovation Is the Mantra

We're in uncharted territory, where the stakes are high and temptation to play small is higher. With a network of collaborators, the faster we experiment, learn, share, and repeat, the faster we'll succeed. We're going up this curve together. The most effective approach to business model innovation is to enable collaborative innovation across functional and company silos.

Magic happens in the interstitial space between silos, disciplines, organizations, and sectors. The word interstitial comes from the Latin "interstitium," which was derived from "inter" (meaning "between") and "sistere" (meaning "to stand"), therefore to stand between. Optimum learning, innovation, problem solving, and value creation happens when we stand between.

To fully realize the potential of the twenty-first century we must get more comfortable and better at standing between. The imperative is to go from interdisciplinary to trans-disciplinary. Only by celebrating the interstitial space between us will we invent new disciplines and fully realize the potential of business model innovation.

And yet we spend most of our time in silos. It is comfortable there. We know the language spoken. We know what is expected and our roles. We know the people who inhabit our silos. There are clear rules dictating our behavior within silos and even clearer rules if we dare to dip our toes into the interstitial space outside of well-marked boundaries. Incentives, performance reviews, and job ladders all reinforce insularity. While technology screams permeability, organization infrastructure and operating norms lean against it. Standing in between anything is often considered a career-limiting move.

Most organizations aren't twenty-first century ready. Industrial-era structures with hierarchical reporting relationships designed around functions will inevitably give way to networked operating models fluidly connecting capabilities both within and outside the organization. Enabling infrastructure and operating norms will celebrate and reinforce interstitial spaces. Standing between disciplines will become the norm rather than the exception. The enabling technology is already here. We don't need to invent anything new. It isn't technology that is in our way. Organizations are stubbornly resistant to change and hesitant to fully explore interstitial spaces. Organizations will either transform themselves to capitalize on the value in interstitial spaces or they will be disrupted in the market by others that do. And for those leaders who think they can wait it out, you can't, the transition has already started and its pace is quickening. Just ask the youngest in your organization. Waiting is not a strategy and will fail.

How many capabilities are locked away, underleveraged in organizational or industry silos? Who hasn't suffered a severe case of innovator's envy, coveting access to information and capabilities that seem so tantalizingly close? The barrier business model innovators face is how to access capabilities and to reconfigure them in order to experiment with a new business model. The problem is capabilities are often impossible to access because stakeholders in the current business model are threatened and won't allow it. The biggest opportunities lie in recombining capabilities from across the gray areas between silos. Business model innovation opportunities will only be realized if we think and act more horizontally.

The trick is to leverage collisions of unusual suspects in purposeful ways. Take spies and environmentalists, for instance. News of the CIA reviving its MEDEA (Measurements of Earth Data for Environmental Analysis) program and providing access to data from national intelligence assets for environmental research really got my attention. What a great example of the power and politics of collaborative innovation.

With no security risk, disruption of agency activities, or incremental cost, the CIA has opened up a treasure trove of valuable data to scientists from academia, government, and industry for environmental research. To replicate the capture of this information would be silly and cost-prohibitive, and I was encouraged that the data were being shared to make progress on an important social issue. But then naysayers and politics entered the conversation. Instead of garnering praise for the program, as I would have expected, the CIA was criticized for mission creep.

Admittedly, news of the collaborative program came right on the heels of a U.S. terror threat. Talking heads across cable news accused the CIA of negligence, arguing that sharing data with environmental scientists was a distraction from its core mission of protecting the American public. But the pundits have it wrong. The CIA and all Homeland Security organizations should be doing more, not less, cross-agency collaboration and data sharing. The protection of data, capabilities, and turf has gotten us into the current mess. Perhaps if the focus had been on networking capabilities and sharing data across silos, America would be a safer country today.

In 1986, the Federal Technology Transfer Act created the CRADA (Cooperative Research and Development Agreement) process to enable public-private partnerships around promising government technologies. CRADA may just as well stand for "Can't Really Access Developed Assets." Government rhetoric claims to support technology transfer, but the painful bureaucratic process in place makes it nearly impossible to leverage existing government capabilities. I get a headache just thinking about how hard it is to access the valuable information and data that have been created by government agencies and paid for by taxpayer dollars. Many of these assets could be leveraged to unleash new value and to help make progress on our big social challenges.

Private-sector organizations are similar. We are so busy pedaling the bicycle of today's business models that there is no capacity to explore new ones. The secret sauce of business model innovation is the ability to explore new ways to deliver customer value by combining and recombining capabilities, in and out of the organization, across silos.

One story that sticks with me is from my friend Alexander Tsiaris, founder of Anatomical Travelogue, who has built a successful company creating human anatomy visualization tools to help us better understand health care. When Alexander was starting his digital media business he needed access to hospital MRI equipment. He was willing to pay for access to the equipment during down times to capture the scanned images he transforms into a beautiful art form and health-care education tool. The initial hospitals he asked all said the same thing: We are not in this business and can't provide access. Alexander is persistent and ultimately found willing partners, but it wasn't easy.

This pattern repeats itself over and over. It is not the technology that gets in the way of innovation. It is stubborn humans and organizations resistant to experimentation and change. If we expect to develop new business models we have to look up from our silos and become more comfortable connecting with unusual suspects in order to recombine capabilities in new and better ways to deliver value.

Principle 4. Build Purposeful Networks

Find actionable connections between people and organizations. Don't just come together but strive together. Cocreate possibilities. It's not enough to just collide with more unusual suspects; business model innovation requires the creation of actionable and purposeful networks. We are going to have to explore entirely new organization and operating structures. Industrial-era hierarchical structures just don't lend themselves to building flexible network structures and experimenting with innovative new business models. Maybe we can glean business model innovation ideas and examples from nature.

MIT researcher Neri Oxman is doing exciting work on the notion of form-seeking structures that have big implications for organization design as we move from self-limiting industrial-era structures to self-organizing networked structures. Neri is an innovative architect who plumbs the natural world for ingenious ways to create objects or structures that meld harmoniously with their surroundings. Her vision of design is not rooted in the philosophy of the Industrial Revolution, when the machine became the ultimate model of functionality—many parts working together as an integral whole, a kit of parts. Instead, Oxman's model of design is the biological world, where there are no assemblies or individual components, but mostly tissues made of single materials (like a leaf) redistributed perfectly to achieve balance and functionality.

Oxman's interdisciplinary research initiative, MATERIALECOLOGY, takes a contemplative approach to design. She asks atypical questions. Not what type of building do we want to design, but what behavior do we want to achieve with this space? What human and environmental values will be important and how do we design a structure to accommodate those values? "We're accustomed to thinking in terms of types and typologies," Oxman says. "We begin with specific a-priori high level rules and work toward some desired product. A typical architectural approach is to assume the separation of materials by their functions—steel and cement for support, glass for insulation, and visual connection to the environment."[1] Natural objects, however, are perfectly designed from single materials. Oxman's designs, several of which are now part of the permanent collection at the Museum of Modern Art in New York, strive to imitate that perfection in man-made materials. Oxman's approach is directly relevant to organization and social system design. How can we apply her fresh thinking to creating new form-seeking structures and models designed around the end-user?

After more than twenty years of deploying consulting teams I guess I take for granted the value of quickly forming flexible interdisciplinary teams to work on specific challenges and opportunities. It seems intuitive and obvious that project teams should be organized around the customer, comprised of the diverse talent needed for the work at hand regardless of what silo or organization function individuals come from. No organization boundaries should ever be allowed to come between the customer and delivering value. Customer-facing team effectiveness is all that matters. Compensation and promotion opportunities must be aligned with customer value delivery.

Over many years as a road warrior consultant, client executives would observe with envy the way consulting teams were easily formed and reformed across silos. Executives would often express a desire that their organizations could work as effectively across functional boundaries. While they wished for a more flexible organization, most were stuck in an industrial-era paradigm and unable to change.

---

[1] From "The Broken Model Theory of Innovation." See the Neri Oxman profile in the BIF Innovation Story Studio.

Most large organizations—including both product and service companies—are stuck in top down functional organizations with entrenched silos. The silos are impermeable and efforts to implement horizontal processes cutting across the organization are always burdened by loyalties and incentives that reinforce vertical affiliations. Interdisciplinary project teams are too slow to come together and often dysfunctional as team members struggle to figure out roles, expectations, and implications of being too far removed from functional homes and bosses.

Industrial-era organization structures are getting in the way of innovation. They are too rigid and unable to seek the networked forms necessary to deliver value to customers in the twenty-first century. The customer is waiting. We need new organization structures and approaches that are form seeking in order to better meet customer needs.

Another interesting example in nature that can teach us about business model innovation comes from observing the social behavior of honeybees. Who hasn't been riveted by devastating stories of colony collapse? This is serious stuff. From a honeybee's perspective, watching 35 percent of your fellow *Apis mellifera* get wiped out is no joke. From a human perspective, think of it this way—one out of every three mouthfuls of food we eat is dependent on honeybee pollination. Bees are responsible for about $15 billion in U.S. agricultural crop value. Colony collapse really matters. It's worth paying attention to bees.

The term colony collapse disorder was first applied to a drastic rise in the number of honeybee disappearances in 2006. It's an eerie phenomenon where one day worker bees swarm together in great numbers and the next they are gone—they just disappear, leaving behind an empty hive. It's not as if they leave to join another colony. They leave to die alone and dispersed, which is strange given the social nature of honeybees. Scientists have been working feverishly to determine the etiology of colony collapse disorder.

Turns out that researchers collaborating from academia and the military think they have found the answer. I am a sucker for a good collaborative innovation story where unusual suspects tag team across silos to solve a problem that neither of them could solve on their own. This one is a classic. Army scientists in Maryland working with academic entomologists in Montana solved the mystery. They applied proteomics-based pathogen screening tools to identify a co-infection comprised of both a virus and a fungus. They found the combination of pathogens in all of the collapsed colonies they tested. Hopefully their findings will lead to pathogen mitigation strategies, dramatically reducing the incidence of colony collapse disorder.

While I am glad the mystery is solved, I can't help asking, what is it about organizing in colonies that prevents bees from innovating themselves? And closer to home, aren't bee colonies like hierarchical corporate structures? Maybe understanding the social behavior of bees in their colonies will help us understand why corporate structures are also vulnerable to colony collapse.

Honeybees are social insects. A honeybee colony is comprised of thousands of bees that cooperate in regimented ways on the day-to-day tasks of nest building, food collection, and brood rearing (substitute here your organization's core processes). Each member of the colony has a very specific task to perform (job descriptions). There is typically one queen bee (CEO), several hundred sycophantic drones (management), and thousands of worker bees (aka, worker bees). Social organizations within a bee colony closely resemble those of a corporation. Each bee has a rigidly specific function. Communication systems are elaborate. I particularly like the "waggle dance" (staff meetings) bees use to communicate assignments and division of labor. Bees are big into seniority, assigning specific tasks based on age, not performance. Scale is everything, with efficiency increasing in direct proportion to colony size. Sound familiar?

It's no wonder bee colonies are unable to adapt and innovate when faced with a threat like colony collapse. They are hierarchical execution machines just like corporations. Flexibility, experimentation, and resiliency don't come to mind. It's not as if bee colonies haven't built up elaborate defense mechanisms to protect against outside threats. There are stingers, elegant hives (including walls varnished with herbicides), and posted guards complete with alarm pheromones. The colony's defenses work fine until an unexpected disruption like the double whammy of a combined virus and fungus brings on colony collapse disorder. The colony is helpless and is quickly destroyed. Does this sound analogous to the Pony Express disrupted by the invention of the telegraph, RCA blindsided by the integrated circuit, and Blockbuster brought to its knees by Netflix?

Hierarchical colonies (organizations) are not designed for innovation, flexibility, or resiliency. Perhaps avoiding colony collapse requires a hybrid organization structure, part colony and part network. A hierarchical core designed for operating efficiency and scale connected to a network structure designed for adaptation, experimentation, and innovation. They're not mutually exclusive structures. With the half-life of business models declining, R&D for new business models is imperative. The twenty-first century requires hybrid structures, one to pedal the bicycle of today's business model and another one to design, prototype, and experiment with new models, especially those with the potential to disrupt current models.

If our current organizations are to avoid colony collapse syndrome, it's worth paying attention to bees.

Principle 5. Together, We Can Design Our Future

Believe in the power of design. Through it, we will chart the landscape of possibility—designing, testing, and prototyping new terrain. Be a market maker rather than a share taker.

Business model innovators are always seeking out places and events with a strong design vibe. They love to hang around really smart design thinkers in hopes that some of it will rub off. I am convinced that design thinking and process is a key enabler of business model innovation, so I have been hanging out with lots of design types. If you hang around enough designers you immediately get pulled into their active conversation about design's place in the innovation narrative. After participating in many of these conversations I am left with a strong sense that the design community needs to move on from the incessant argument over the importance of design thinking and process. It is time to claim victory. Get over it. The argument is boring. Design is important. We stipulate that design is about more than sexy products. We get that design is about delivering a compelling customer experience. We know that business model innovation is fundamentally about designing new ways to create, deliver, and capture value. Now, can we get on with putting design thinking and process to work to enable business model innovation?

No more books are needed to convince us that design thinking and process are a priority. They are important tools. If you want to convince us, stop talking about design thinking, and start putting it to work to mobilize new business models, transform customer experiences, and enable real systems change. Business model innovation requires a strong design vibe that leads to trying more stuff and putting the tools to work rather than the navel gazing of today's design thinking debate. It is time to move the design conversation to a new, actionable, place.

We need more mad designers focused on customer experience and business model innovation. If you don't have design talent in your organization doing more than product and website design you are making a mistake. Whether you are interested in business model innovation or not, you should be leveraging design thinking and process to improve your customer experience. It is a requirement for business model innovation. In fact, maybe we need to bang together the heads of mad scientists and mad designers.

If we are waiting for lengthy business plans with detailed financial analysis and randomized double blind studies to tell us if a new business model is viable, we will be waiting a very long time. That is not how business model innovation works. It takes passionate exploration, which is more iterative than traditional scientific methodology. It takes design thinking and process combined with powerful storytelling to create novel business models. We need to try more stuff, and design thinking and process can help.

I am reminded of a recent innovation talk I was asked to give at a conference on the business of aging. It was a great event attended by many innovators from across the public and private sector. Attendees all shared a passion for focusing innovation on the opportunity emerging as the silver tsunami of an aging global population rapidly approaches. I shared my point of view on the need to do R&D for new business models and systems and our work at the Business Innovation Factory (BIF), where we have an Elder Experience Lab to do real world experimentation for new business models and systems to transform the elder experience. As I always do, I blathered on about design and storytelling tools as the key enablers to system change, in this case developing age-friendly environments and communities.

The reaction was largely positive, but during a panel discussion I was reminded that many are still stuck on a perceived conflict between design thinking and analytical thinking, between design process and scientific method. They are not mutually exclusive. We need to apply our opposable minds to borrow from both approaches to design new systems while measuring what works and is most likely to scale.

I was asked by the conference organizers what I thought would be the most important innovation to enable an age-friendly society by 2020. I replied that perhaps the most important innovation for an age-friendly society doesn't require inventing anything new at all. Maybe it just requires all of us to reexamine our assumptions about the elder experience and ways to enhance it. Innovation is a better way to deliver value; in this case, designing environments and systems that enable elders to age in their own homes and communities with dignity. The innovation may be nothing fancier than bringing the voice of elders directly into the conversation and designing a better experience recombining existing capabilities and assets in new ways to better serve their needs.

Most of today's innovation conversation is through the lens of the institutions that comprise the current elder care system. The elder's voice is missing. Tweaking the current system will not work. Adding technology to the current system will not work either. We need to design new system approaches to enhance the elder experience and to prepare for the imminent silver tsunami of baby boomers that will bring a completely new set of expectations and desires to the age-friendly conversation.

It is not technology that is getting in our way. We have more technology available to us then we know how to absorb. Rather than applying technology in a sustaining way to try and improve the current institutionally-based elder care system, we need to experiment with technology as a disrupter to enable new system approaches that enable elders to age in place. We need system-level innovation designed around the elder to create environments and care models that enable a more age-friendly society.

It is odd for me to represent design thinking and process in the debate when my education and training is as a scientist and MBA. The reason I hang around so many smart designers is that I don't think the old tricks alone will enable the business model innovation and system change we need. We need to borrow from both approaches to pave a new way. It is messy but necessary. Let's bring together the mad scientists and mad designers and see what happens.

5 Inspire: We Do What We Are Passionate About

I nnovators are epic optimists, fueled by a passion and conviction to always find a better way. We must inspire them daily with portraits of possibilities.

Principle 6. Stories Can Change the World

Stories are magical. They connect us and carry us into the future. Create new stories every day. Make them beautiful and bring them to listeners who are in search of them. Together, you will narrate the future. "Facts are facts, but stories are who we are, how we learn, and what it all means," says my friend Alan Webber, cofounder of Fast Company and author of *Rules of Thumb*. He has it exactly right. Storytelling is the most important tool for any innovator. It is the best way to create emotional connections to your ideas and innovations. I don't know if the neuroscience of storytelling is well understood, but somehow effective stories bypass the logic centers in our brains and connect directly with our emotions. Sharing stories is the way to create a network of passionate supporters that can help spread ideas and make them a reality. We remember stories. We relate to stories and they compel us to action. Storytelling is a critical element of any successful business model innovation effort.

Storytelling is a core value at the Business Innovation Factory (BIF). We believe that advancing our mission to enable system change in health care, education, energy, and entrepreneurship is critically dependant on our ability to create, package, and share stories from our work. Everything we do is about storytelling and our Innovation Story Studio is one of BIF's most important capabilities. By openly sharing stories about the process and output of BIF's work, we are strengthening our community of innovators and becoming more purposeful with every new story. Storytelling isn't the same as traditional push marketing and communication. It isn't about tying a ribbon on the outcomes of a successful project and pushing out core messages and collateral material to target audiences. Storytelling is about sharing the messy process and personal narrative of generative development while it is happening in a transparent way. It is about sharing the story of the process so that others can participate in the story and help to improve it. It is a way to create emotional connections to the work while it is happening so that when an exciting new business model emerges there are already passionate supporters that want to help bring more people in to engage in the story and commit to its success.

It is no surprise that BIF's annual Collaborative Innovation Summit, which takes place every September in Providence, Rhode Island, is all about storytelling. The summit is two days of total immersion in bone jarring, compelling, and personal stories of innovation. The stories are so wonderfully eclectic as to defy any attempt at grouping them in convenient buckets. The emotive storytellers dare us every year to hone our pattern recognition and sense-making skills.

I will never forget meeting with my friend and mentor Richard Saul Wurman (RSW) to get his advice prior to our first summit in 2004. As an innovation junkie it doesn't get any better than having RSW as a mentor. He founded TED, for heaven's sake. I went to the meeting prepared with an approach that I had worked on for weeks. As an MBA, of course I had a matrix, with speakers organized by theme. RSW heard me out and could only shake his head, saying, Saul you have a lot to learn about how to create an emotional connection with an audience. He patiently told me to throw away the matrix. He said it was as simple as inviting people to a dinner party. Ask speakers that you want to have dinner with to share a personal story that you are selfishly interested in and invite others to listen in.

I love RSW for that advice. That is exactly what we do. No Power-Point presentations, no matrix, just stories. One glorious story after another in no particular order, from storytellers (not speakers) sharing personal and raw insights about what innovation means to them. After about four to five stories back to back with no boring Q&A to break the rhythm, we take a long break where all of the storytellers and participants can interact, connect, and share their own innovation stories and experiences. No breakouts, flip charts, or prescriptive assignments. It is up to the 400 summit participants to decide what is compelling and which connections are most interesting and valuable. We trust our audience. The most interesting collaborations every year come from connecting unusual suspects that find value in the gray area between their interests and disciplines.

Every year the magical Trinity Rep theatre in Providence, where we hold the summit, is overflowing with a collective self-awareness that we are always missing something and an obsession for discovery, making us open to exploring the gray areas between our silos, disciplines, and organizational boundaries. Our culture media is a perfect mix of rapid-fire provocative storytellers, the dissonance of seemingly unrelated innovation stories, and knowing we are among fellow innovators sharing a common quest. The environment is an ideal communal petri dish in which to grow connections and insights. Incubation is spontaneous and palpable. It is as if there are chemi-luminescent tags lighting a synaptic path networking us together. It is an electric feeling of potential and possibilities. It is remarkable, exhilarating, and exhausting. Of course, I am biased but it's my book! Mashable has called the BIF summit one of the top seven places to watch great minds in action. You should come.

Every year one of my favorite things to do is connect with each of the thirty or so storytellers to discuss the upcoming summit and their stories. Many of the insights in this book come from my interaction with over 200 inspiring innovation storytellers and over 2,000 like-minded innovation junkies who have participated in the summit. Talk about a kid in a candy store. To talk with each of these innovators is inspiring and a great joy. These innovators are asked to give speeches all the time. Many of them have written books and do speaking tours. They all have PowerPoint presentations in the drawer and a stock speech they can give in their sleep, which they are not allowed to use at a BIF summit.

I always find our storyteller's reactions interesting when they discuss preparations for sharing a story versus giving a speech. They all say that it's far more interesting and challenging to tell a story than to give a speech. Regardless of their fame on the speaking circuit, there is always trepidation in their voices when we discuss their stories. Every storyteller over the years has said that they are excited to hear the stories from the other storytellers and will be glad when they are done sharing their own. That is why they take the gig. It is a refreshing break from the grind of the speaking circuit. Storytelling is harder but more personally rewarding.

The secret of effective storytelling is to trust the audience to determine for itself the most relevant patterns, what connections are most valuable, and which stories most energizing. Seems so basic, yet it is our nature to be prescriptive, to tell people what they are supposed to get out of an event, what conclusions they are supposed to reach, who they should be collaborating with, and what they should be working on. Nonsense. That is so limiting and boring. If you trust the audience to create the insights and connections that make sense to them and provide an environment that is conducive to connecting the unusual suspects and ideas, the magic will happen. My friend and storytelling expert Steve Denning says, "People think in stories, communicate in stories, even dream in stories. If you want to get anything done in an organization, you need to know how to use story to move people." I agree with Steve; stories can change the world, they can certainly help to change a business model, and storytelling is the way to make it happen.

Principle 7. Make Systems-Level Thinking Sexy

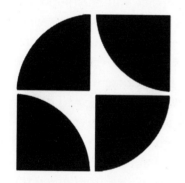

You are choosing a path that can be complex, nerdy, difficult, and trying. Make it an adventure of epic proportions. Systems-level thinking is the new cool. Improving an existing business model can often be accomplished by focusing narrowly on individual components of the model as long as solutions don't require other parts of the business model to change. Business model innovation requires the ability to work on all of the parts simultaneously. It requires the ability to combine and recombine capabilities, even those that are not within the four walls of your organization. It requires systems-level thinking and action. The most interesting new business models require an even broader perspective outside of the confines of traditional industry boundaries.

Systems-level thinking gives most people a big headache. It is far easier to work on the things that we can control and not to imagine what would be possible if we could experiment to include things that we don't believe we can access, influence, or control. Systems-level thinking helps us to imagine new business models that leverage capabilities controlled by functions outside of our own, even capabilities controlled by other organizations entirely. Sorry to disappoint, but business model innovation isn't easy. It has enormous upside potential but requires the ability to take a fresh systems-level view. It starts by changing your perspective and examining new opportunities to create, deliver, and capture value that will only be seen by putting the lens of your current business model aside. To make business model innovation an ongoing strategic imperative requires making systems-level thinking sexy.

However tempting it is to focus exclusively on squeezing more value from your current business model, for business model innovation squeezing harder won't work. Consider a toothpaste tube.

Here's the thing about toothpaste tubes. You can squeeze all you want on one part of the tube and the toothpaste will only pop up in another part of the tube. Industry clusters and social systems work much the same way. The best business model innovation opportunities require systems thinking and systems solutions. Existing industry systems have evolved over a long time. Current players and competitors within the system work hard year after year to deliver value, improve their position, and create sustained incremental improvements. System tweaks are not enough to remain competitive given the risk of disruption from new competitors who don't play by current industry rules. Every industry is at risk from emerging disrupters who are redefining traditional industry boundaries. All organizations are going to have to learn how to create new toothpaste tubes or risk being disrupted by others who will. Business model innovation is not about squeezing harder on different parts of the current toothpaste tube. We need more market makers. Business model innovators are market makers more than share takers. We need to design and experiment with new systems-level solutions.

Everyone loves to point fingers at the other players in the system as the cause of the problem. Health care is a classic example. Observing our health care system today is like watching an intense rugby scrum that is moving in slow motion, hoping the ball will pop out—finger pointing and incessant public policy debates galore. We love to admire the problems: It is the cost of drugs that is killing us. It is the high-cost hospitals that are the problem. It is the insurance companies that are in the way of change. Doctors are the ones who are resisting change. If only the government would get its act together. If only patients would take more responsibility for their care. It goes on and on.

In education, the same movie is playing with different actors. It's the unions that are getting in the way. Teachers are resisting change in the classroom. Administrators don't understand what is going on in the classroom. Parents are not engaged. Public policymakers can't make up their minds. If only private sector companies were more engaged. Students are unruly, undisciplined, and disrespectful. Everyone is blamed and nothing changes.

Call me a cynic, but I've seen and participated in many innovation initiatives that are trying to create systems-level changes within health care and education. And some of them have indeed succeeded in creating incremental value. But what we need are more disrupters and systems-level game changers. The problem is that great ideas coming from one silo are tried but quickly bump into the other silos and constraints of the system. Promising new solutions squeezes on one part of the toothpaste tube only to learn that when you squeeze on one part of the tube it just pops up in another. We need safe environments to design and experiment with new toothpaste tubes or systems.

Consumers, citizens, patients, and students should be at the center of system redesign efforts. Business model innovators will imagine new system approaches, including leveraging technology in more disruptive ways to significantly improve how value is delivered from current business model approaches. We need to experiment at the systems level, trying new approaches to see what works. Disrupters have proven that business model innovation works in the education industry at the school level, with hundreds of successful charter schools across the country and an explosion in online learning platforms. Now we need to experiment at the district, region, and state levels to test new student-centered system approaches that are not constrained by the way the current system operates. That is the only way we are going to learn which new business models can deliver value to the student at scale. The same thing is true in the health-care industry. We need to design and test patient-centered system approaches that are more about well care than about sick care. We can't get there by playing at the margins of today's system. Squeezing today's toothpaste tubes harder will not work.

Principle 8. Transformation Is Itself a Creative Act

Imagination has moved beyond the artist's studio and into the C-Suite. Engage in the creative practice of designing the core models that drive businesses, institutions, industries, and cultures. Dismiss your assumptions because nothing is absolute.

Business model innovation is less about analysis and planning and more about generating and trying new approaches to see what works. Incremental improvements require going from knowing to doing. Transformation requires going from doing to knowing. Business model innovation is a generative act unleashed by creativity.

Again, it's worth thinking about regeneration and learning from examples found in nature. While it is common knowledge, it still amazes me that salamanders can regenerate body parts, including their tails, upper and lower jaws, eyes, and hearts. Yet mammals, including humans, can't. Salamanders are the highest order of animals capable of regeneration. Do mammals know something that salamanders don't? Cosmetic surgery, implants, and promising regenerative medicine research aside, we humans are stuck with the body parts we are dealt for now.

I wonder if our inability to regenerate at the biological scale also impedes our ability to regenerate at the business model, industry, and social system scale. It seems obvious that they all need serious regeneration. Existing business models, industry sectors, and social systems have evolved over a long period of time, were built to support an industrial era that is long gone, and have built up incredible mechanisms to resist and prevent needed change. It is not technology that is getting in the way of business model innovation, industry transformation, and social system change. It is humans and the organizations we live in. Why are humans so incapable of regeneration at any scale?

Maybe understanding the biology of regeneration can provide insight. Salamanders can regenerate injured body parts because evolution has enabled them to immediately unleash stem-like cells to a wound site when damage is detected. When salamanders are wounded, skin, bone, muscle, and blood vessels at the site revert to their undifferentiated state. In essence, they go back to an embryonic state and start all over again, making regeneration possible. Humans took a different evolutionary path.

Turns out the human evolutionary pathway traded off regeneration in favor of tumor suppression. In order to decrease the risk of cancer and increase longevity, our mammalian ancestors selected against regeneration. The theory is that the rapid cell division required for regeneration looks to our bodies a lot like the unchecked growth of cancer. Because our longevity makes us vulnerable to accumulated DNA mutations, we've evolved a kind of molecular brake to keep tumors at bay. I can't speak for humankind, but it seems like the right trade-off to me. Unlike salamanders, when mammals lose a limb the body's reaction is to release cells to the site that become scar tissue. Current stem cell research is promising and offers the future potential for a work-around to enable regeneration without turning off the molecular brake that prevents tumor formation and progression.

Tissue generation and regenerative medicine are both exciting fields to watch.

I think there are parallels at the business model, industry sector, and social system scale. Each has evolved over a long period of time, selecting for traits that maximize longevity. Let's give them the benefit of the doubt and say they are all well-intentioned and pedaling very hard to deliver value. The truth is they are no longer positioned to deliver value the way we want and need them to. We all know there is a better way. The twenty-first century screams for regeneration and yet the best we seem to be able to do is tweak current models and to leverage technology in a sustaining way to coax more life out of business models and systems that are not sustainable. The evolutionary pathway for our current business models and social systems seems to have traded off regeneration in favor of innovation suppression. I know it seems extreme to equate innovation to a cancerous cell in an organization or social system. But hey, I have seen and worked in many organizations and systems, in both the public and private sectors, which have built up incredible defenses to insulate and protect themselves from innovation and change. Tell me you haven't experienced the same thing? Our social systems have evolved antibodies to attack and wear down innovators. Organization and system leaders fear metastasis of disruptive technologies and seeds of change. They have established an armamentarium of tools to resist and block regeneration.

We don't need more tweaks. We need system regeneration fueled by imagination and creativity. Just like tissue engineering and stem cell research is opening up the possibility of regeneration at a biological scale, we need to leverage social media and purposeful networks of innovators to enable regeneration at the business model and social system scale. We must design, prototype, and test new solutions in the real world to determine what works and can scale. Transformation is itself a creative act. Let's unleash the newt within.

Principle 9. Passion Rules—Exceed Your Own Expectations

Let loose your passion, and it will fuel you to epic proportions. Ask more of yourself and your communities of practice. Take risks with confidence. Up the ante, you are capable beyond your imagination.

How many times since President Kennedy rallied the collective passion of our nation to send a man safely to the moon have you heard someone say, "Where is our moon mission? Where is our passion?" We commit to our passions. We invest our minds, our time, and our resources in passions and passionate people. We will create a more prosperous economy and stronger companies and communities when we enable connections between passionate people and create an environment where innovators can more easily pursue their passions. Knowledge and networks are important enablers, but passion is the secret sauce. We need to move from a knowledge-based economy to a passion-based economy. Who gets excited about a knowledge-based economy? Where is the passion? I have spent a ton of time and effort to rally the troops. If I am honest, people just haven't connected emotionally. The knowledge-based economy has given us the tools we need but has fallen short in solving the real issues of our time, including health care, education, energy independence, and an economy with entrepreneurship at its core. These are all systems issues that will require systems solutions. Systems-level innovation requires passionate leaders and organizations that are committed to a cause. Passion-based organizations stop at nothing to accomplish their goals and are able to attract people and resources to their causes. A passion economy can arise that unleashes both a new era of prosperity and solutions for the big issues of our time.

Without passion, business model innovation ideas will rapidly become tweaks. My friend Jana Eggers, who I first met when she ran the Innovation Lab at Intuit and now is the vice president of product management and marketing for Blackbaud, once shared her marathon and iron man competition schedule with me. I was exhausted just thinking about it. "It turned into a passion," she said. "I go overboard on passion." That got me thinking. Over all of my years as an innovation junkie, the common denominator, among the innovators I have connected with and the most successful enterprises I have observed and worked with, is passion. They started with a passion or cause and then organized around it to make it happen. Not the other way around.

I first met the famous ocean explorer, *Titanic* discoverer Bob Ballard, in his office at the Mystic Aquarium. I will never forget his passion. He called me over to a wall that was a huge topographic map of the ocean floor. We sat on the floor in front of the map and Bob took me on a tour of the ocean's many mysteries. He shared with me his infectious passion to transform education and to get kids excited about science again by making the ocean's secrets accessible to every school-age child.

I had an identical experience at dinner with Dean Kamen when he shared his passion with me for getting every school-age child involved in his FIRST Robotics program. I went to the finals one year and was blown away that it filled the Georgia Dome with motivated kids from around the world learning math and science experientially by competing in a fun robotics competition. Parents and sponsors were screaming in the stands. If you closed your eyes you would have thought you were at a sold-out sports event. Imagine what we could accomplish if we reinforced and supported science competitions the way we support sports.

I see the same passion in many business leaders too. Tony Hsieh of Zappos, Jason Fried at 37 Signals, and Shai Agassi with Better Place, just to name a few. They are building enterprises based on a passion and clear point-of-view. They are masters at attracting interest and participation in their passions. They all are active collaborators always looking to extend their ideas and networks. Companies built around a passion like these examples do not need traditional marketing departments. Their employees and customers buy in to the cause and become the marketing and advertising department. It is amazing to see how they attract new ideas, employees, and customers by leveraging social network platforms to share their passion openly with others.

My friend and BIF advisor Bill Taylor, founder of Fast Company and author of *Mavericks at Work* and *Practically Radical* says it well: "It's about having a distinctive point-of-view and a passion for where your company and industry can and should be going." As I think about the successful leaders that I have connected with through our work at BIF they all share the same attribute: a passion for their cause. It is the same for leaders of both for-profit and non-profit business models. I push the idea even further to suggest that the biggest value-creating ideas will be found in the gray areas between sectors, silos, and disciplines. We need passionate leaders that can get below the buzzwords of public-private partnerships to enable system-level innovation in the areas that matter the most. Both the public and private sector needs it to happen and both will benefit from a shift toward a passion-based economy.

In his book *Hot, Flat, and Crowded*, Tom Friedman calls for an energy revolution: "it requires lots of teamwork and collaboration among business, government, and academe; it requires thousands of people working in their garages, trying thousands of things" he writes.[1] In addition to the energy revolution, I think we need a similar passion-driven revolution in health care and education. A passion-driven economy with a focus on areas of critical social needs will attract ideas, innovators, and resources to create new systems-level solutions to deliver value to the consumer patient, student, and citizen. It will also strengthen our economy, creating prosperity and new job opportunities.

---

[1] Thomas L. Friedman, *Hot, Flat, and Crowded* (New York: Farrar, Straus and Giroux, 2008), 214.

If your organization is blindly vested in the way you do business today, it is a good time to explore and test new business models with a clear passion at the core. If your organization is determined to resist change, move out of the way because the wisdom of crowds has learned how to mobilize behind a compelling passion. These new purposeful networks will not be stopped.

Principle 10. Be Inspiration Accelerators

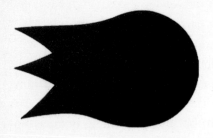

It happens less and less in a world of apathy. Inspire. Inspire many. But inspire toward the end game: transformation.

I am often asked, what is the single most important thing holding our economy back? Without hesitation I answer, our psychology is bad and negativism is getting in the way. We have allowed cynicism to slow progress, growth, and innovation. I am as cynical as anyone. Where I live in New England we are born with a well-developed cynical streak. In my home state of Rhode Island we have taken the art of cynicism to entirely new heights. I am convinced we won't climb out of this economic mess until we become more confident in ourselves, our communities, and our opportunities. Psychology matters. A strong innovation economy creating higher wage jobs results from the decisions made every day by organization leaders and entrepreneurs. It is the sum total of these decisions on the margin to hire one additional employee or to invest one additional dollar which determine the trajectory of our economy. While many factors influence these choices, in the end it comes down to psychology or confidence. We must find a way to move beyond our cynicism.

The imperative is to unleash the animal spirits. John Maynard Keynes had it right in his book, *The General Theory of Employment, Interest, and Money*, when he described animal spirits as the emotion that influences human behavior measured in terms of consumer confidence. Keynes got the math right. Positive activities depend on spontaneous optimism rather than mathematical expectations. Our decisions to do something positive can only be taken as the result of animal spirits, a spontaneous urge to action rather than inaction, and not as the outcome of a weighted average of quantitative benefits multiplied by quantitative probabilities. Amen.

Keynes stood on the shoulders of earlier philosophers who also asserted that psychology matters. David Hume, one of the most important historical contributors to Western philosophy, has been credited with laying the foundation for cognitive science. In his seminal work, *A Treatise of Human Nature*, Hume lays out his framework for a naturalistic science of man that examines the psychological basis of human nature. His views in 1739 were heretical and in direct opposition to the prevailing views of the rationalists, exemplified by Descartes. Hume concluded that belief rather than reason governed human behavior. I love Hume's famous quote, "Reason is, and ought only to be the slave of the passions."

Before accusing me of being Polyanna-ish (optimist for sure) or having my head stuck in a history book (only partially stuck), consider what is going on around you. Everybody is pointing at everybody else. It's the government's fault. It's the big bad industrial complex. There aren't enough resources to go around. Democrats and Republicans are beating each other up incessantly while nothing changes (a pox on both of their houses). Change is hard. Life isn't fair. And so it goes. Add your barriers and excuses here. Can we move beyond admiring the problem now? How we love to admire the problem. Enough already.

We have an incredible opportunity in front of us. We must overcome our cynicism and bring passion to the fore as we optimistically try more stuff. Sure there are challenges, but we live in a technology-rich era with an unprecedented opportunity to enable purposeful networks focused on solving the big issues of day. Clay Shirky has it right in his books, *Here Comes Everybody* and *Cognitive Surplus*. We are connected, communicating, and leveraging social media platforms in powerful new ways. Collectively we are blessed with a cognitive surplus that is huge, obvious, and accessible to solve real-world problems and redefine how value is created, delivered, and captured. We just need to get on with it. It is time to stop admiring the problem. The biggest obstacle in our way is a negative psychology and lack of confidence to act. Time to unleash the animal spirits.

In his book *Drive*, Dan Pink crystallized my lifelong instinct that our thinking about motivation and incentives is out of sync with the possibilities of the twenty-first century. It is time to reboot motivation. The twentieth century was all about management. The North Star was how to get more people to go through the motions efficiently. Seeking personal meaning in work was a distraction. The best workers follow the rules, work hard, and smile. Work boiled down to an algorithm rendering out any creativity or autonomy. Fulfillment and empowerment were HR buzzwords and the "soft stuff" relegated to off-site retreats that did not get in the way of real work. Incentives in the industrial era were all about carrots and sticks. Motivation was based solely on external factors including compensation, title, office, and promotion opportunities.

Early in my consulting career I worked for a boutique firm that specialized in sales force incentive compensation programs. I was consistently amazed by the gaping disconnect between the home office that inevitably overengineered its goal-setting and compensation practices and the actual behavior out in the sales territory. Sales representatives made quick work of these elegant plans, figuring out how to game the system to optimize earnings. They cherry-picked the incentive plans based on experience, likelihood of earning a payout, and implications for the following year. The annual dance was demotivating and rarely resulted in self-directed effort to maximize either the short- or long-term value of customer relationships within a sales territory.

I have observed legions of managers attempting to manipulate the dials of industrial-era tools to optimize the output of employees.

While it was clear to me this approach sucked the meaning, autonomy, and motivation out of work for most employees, it had the unfortunate advantage of delivering short-term business results, until it didn't. The game changed when computers began to replace people doing repeatable work tasks. Technology also enabled repeatable work that still requires human involvement to move to lower-cost locations. If it can be reduced to an algorithm, it can either be virtualized or moved. This work is dehumanizing and uninteresting. Industrial-era work has left the United States and it is not coming back. The work remaining requires both a new set of twenty-first century skills and a new approach to incentives and performance management.

In *Drive*, Dan Pink sounds the clarion call for a new motivation paradigm. He proclaims, "This era doesn't call for better management. It calls for a renaissance of self-direction. Carrots and sticks don't work in an innovation economy that values heuristic over algorithmic tasks."[2] Industrial-era incentives won't work. Today we need people who are self-directed, work effectively in diverse teams, and can thrive with complex tasks that require flexible thinking and approaches. We need to reboot motivation thinking to align the exciting work of a new century with people who have longed to find meaning in their work and contribute their full potential and passion to it. Self-determination theory argues that we have three innate psychological needs: competence, autonomy, and relatedness. Organizations must realign their human capital strategies and practices to these needs. Intrinsic motivation is what counts today and most companies are still focused on managing external motivation factors. For most organizations the required change will not be a tweak but a transformation of current HR operating models.

It is time to get on with it. As Pink points out in *Drive*, the first decade of the twenty-first century was a staggering underachievement

---

[2] Daniel H. Pink, *Drive* (New York: Riverhead Books, 2009), 90.

in business, technology, and social progress. We have an incredible opportunity for innovation ahead of us, but it will require a new motivation paradigm and tools to unleash the vast reservoir of global talent. People are driven by purpose, passion, and meaning and it is about time we created a generation of leadership that gets it. Be an inspiration accelerator.

6 Transform: Incremental Change Isn't Working

Together, we are designing the future. The past is not our reference point; tweaks won't do. We must create a wholly new vision and experiment our way to its emergence.

Principle 11. Tweaks Won't Do It

Incrementalism won't invent the future. Stay clear, focused, and certain of the goal—transformational change. Never back down and never compromise.

Transformation is more about creating next practices than implementing best practices. Everyone bows down to the all-important benchmark. How many times have you heard someone say, "You only get what you measure"? Most organizations commit to identifying and measuring performance against industry best practice. Many have recognized the value of looking outside of their industry for practices that might provide a source of competitive advantage. Adopting existing best practice makes sense if you want to improve the performance of your current business model. Going beyond the limits of your current business model requires a network-enabled capability to do R&D for new business models. The imperative is to build on best practices to explore and develop next practices. Business model innovation is about creating next practices.

Understanding best practices and applying them to increase business model productivity is an essential capability for all organizations. It is no surprise most companies benchmark their performance against existing industry best practice. It doesn't take long to exhaust the library of best practices in any given industry. Confining exploration to only your own industry for best practices is too limiting. New sources of competitive advantage are far more likely to come from observing and adopting best practices in completely unrelated industries. All leaders should spend more discretionary time outside of their industry, discipline, and sector. There is more to learn from unusual suspects who bring fresh and different perspectives than from the ideas circulated and recirculated among the usual suspects. The big and important value-creating opportunities will most likely be found in the gray areas between the silos we inhabit. Get out more.

Best practices are necessary but not sufficient. Business models don't last as long as they used to. Leaders must identify and experiment with next practices. Next practices enable new ways to deliver customer value. Next practices are better ways to combine and network capabilities that change the value equation of your organization. Organizations should always be developing a portfolio of next practices that recombine capabilities to find new ways to deliver value. Leaders should design and test new business models unconstrained by the current business or industry model.

It is not best practices, but next practices that will sustain your organization on a strong growth trajectory. While you continue to pedal the bicycle of today's business model, make sure that no less than 10 percent of your time and resources are dedicated to exploring new business models and developing next practices.

We can learn by observing two recent Olympic stars. What's your Double McTwist 1260? Are you more like the Olympic snowboarder Shaun White or figure skater Evan Lysacek? Both brought home Olympic gold in 2010 but each took a different path to the podium. Evan took the less risky path, avoiding a quad jump in his final performance, while Shaun did his signature risky move, a back-to-back double cork, under the pressure of an Olympic medal competition. Both Evan and Shaun were awesome with performances that captured the spirit of Olympic competition and gave Americans a source of great national pride. Evan nailed the fundamentals, avoiding mistakes, and beat out a competitor who attempted a bigger, more risky move and missed. Shaun was competing for more than the gold medal. He is reinventing his sport and setting a higher standard that all other competitors are left trying to emulate. Which athlete will be more memorable? Which path do you take to the medal stand?

I don't want to take anything away from Evan Lysacek. He nailed his long routine and I loved watching his gold medal performance. There had been a lot of hype about whether it was possible to win the gold without successfully landing a quad. The quadruple jump with four twists in the air has been part of the Olympic skating competition since 1988, when Canadian Kurt Browning first landed one. In the run-up to the Vancouver games supporters of Yevgeny Plushenko, the 2006 gold medal winner in Turin, were vocal about the need to successfully land a quad to even be considered for the gold medal. Evan was buying none of it. He didn't do a quad while winning the 2009 World Championships and had no intention of adding the risky move to his Olympic routine. It worked. He was flawless in his quest for gold while Plushenko landed the quad hard and ended up with the silver medal. By being excellent at the fundamentals during his performance and not attempting the risky move, Evan's strategy produced a well-deserved gold medal for him and the first for an American male figure skater since Brian Boitano in 1988.

In snowboarding, the corollary to a quad jump in figure skating is the back-to-back double cork. You have to love the names of these moves. The best I can explain, a double cork is two flips and three rotations (1080 degrees), with a move to grab the snowboard sprinkled in for good measure. Doing them back-to-back is insane and considered a necessary move to be in the hunt for any Olympic medal. For Shaun White, just doing what every other serious competitor is doing in competition is not enough. He is a game changer. He wants to change the sport and to dominate with new moves that keep the competition chasing him. The 2010 Olympics was no different. After Shaun had locked down the gold medal with a great back-to-back double cork move in his first run he then went on in his second run to perform a new signature move that he invented called the Double McTwist 1260. Sounds like a milkshake. This unbelievable move includes two board-over-head flips while making three-and-a-half rotations (1260 degrees). It doesn't sound humanly possible but there was Shaun nailing the move, reinventing his sport under the global spotlight of the Olympics. It was game, set, and match on the spot.

I hold both of these great athletes in high esteem. As a complete klutz I can only enjoy their accomplishments vicariously. A gold medal, regardless of the path taken to earn it, is just plain impressive. But as an innovation junkie I can't help but be more taken with what Shaun White has meant for his sport and the game-changing approach he brings to it. I suspect he will be remembered within and outside of his sport longer than Evan will. Are you more like Evan or Shaun in your work and life? Do you try to be great at the game as it is currently defined or do you attempt to create a new game, one that you can dominate? What's your Double McTwist 1260? Business model innovation is about transformation, not tweaks.

Principle 12. Experiment All the Time

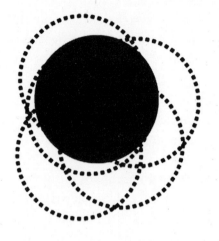

Learn by doing. Constantly test new ideas. Learn, share, and repeat. The world is ever-changing—stay ahead of the curve. Embrace the art of discovery.

We need to try more stuff. Innovation is never about silver bullets. It's about experimentation and doing whatever it takes, even if it means trying 1,000 things, to deliver value. Business model innovation requires a lot more experimentation than we are comfortable with today. Tweaking existing business models won't work. Technology as a sustaining innovation may improve the efficiency of current business models, but will not result in the transformation that we all want and need. We need to learn how to leverage technology for disruptive innovation and to experiment with new business models.

My mantra is "Think Big, Start Small, Scale Fast." The imperative for all innovators is R&D for new business models. We know how to do R&D for new products and technologies. We need to also do R&D for new business models and social systems. We have plenty of technology available to us. We need to learn how to leverage it to enable transformative ways to deliver value. Designing and experimenting with new business models, particularly those that cut across sectors and silos, is the path to the transformation.

Geoffrey Canada, the inspiring founder of the Harlem Children's Zone in New York City, reminds us of the importance of constant experimentation. Everyone wants to know the one thing that makes a program like Harlem Children's Zone successful. What is the silver bullet that will allow the program to be replicated with ease across the country? We are always looking for an easy answer. There is no silver bullet and it is not easy to transform any business model or social system. According to Canada at Harlem Children's Zone, it is doing 1,000 things with passion to help those children succeed. It is about focusing on the customer—in this case, the children within 100 city blocks in Harlem—and doing whatever it takes to help them secure a bright future. There is no one thing. There are a lot of things that were tried, many that didn't work or add value, and a strong appetite for trying new approaches to achieve the goal.

Business model innovation is all about experimentation. It is about combining and recombining capabilities from across silos until something clicks and value is delivered in a new way. It is never just one thing. It starts with a big idea that gets the juices flowing and attracts others with similar passion to the new approach. The big idea has to be translated from the whiteboard to a real-world test bed to demonstrate that the idea is feasible. Starting small and demonstrating progress is key to building credibility and expanding a network of interested stakeholders. An ongoing portfolio of small-scale experiments to fail fast on those without merit and to prioritize those with the potential to scale is critical. Those experiments that demonstrate the feasibility of a new model or approach become candidates for expansion. Scaling fast becomes more likely with the ability to leverage the proof point of a successful real-world experiment and the opportunity to leverage a network of passionate supporters.

We also must get far more comfortable with hacking capabilities. Capabilities are the amino acids of innovation. They are the building blocks that enable value delivery. Innovation is a better way to deliver value and is often the result of repurposing existing capabilities. Locking capabilities into rigid organization structures and proprietary closed systems gets in the way of unleashing new sources of value and solving many of the important challenges of our time. Innovation is about hacking capabilities. Business model innovation happens when we enable random capability collisions, resulting in new and unexpected ways to deliver value.

A good example of the power and potential of hacking capabilities is Microsoft's Kinect. Microsoft introduced Kinect in November 2010 as a product extension to its Xbox franchise. Kinect adds a very cool capability for Xbox game players by getting rid of the handheld game controller and turning players into their own controllers. It lets players "be the controller" with gesture recognition technology. Onscreen menus are navigated by voice and hand waves. Game avatars are manipulated through body gestures. Microsoft and cool haven't been used in the same sentence for a long time. Kinect is cool.

Microsoft predictably launched Kinect with its deeply ingrained proprietary product mind-set. You could buy Kinect as a bundle with an Xbox or as a separate component to attach to an existing Xbox for $150. While Microsoft views Kinect as a product, the global geek community views it as a capability. To geeks, Kinect is a powerful capability screaming to be hacked and repurposed for exciting new uses beyond its use as an Xbox extension. Hackers view Kinect as an interesting voice and gesture recognition platform complete with sophisticated cameras, software, and sensors with the power to detect movement, depth, shape, and position of the human body. What a bargain for only $150. It's a hacker's dream.

And hack they will. A crowd of makers, programmers, roboticists, and other assorted and sundry geeks are exploring what Kinect can enable beyond Microsoft's initial intention. There was even a bounty of $3,000, announced by the founder of a New York City store that sells supplies for experimental hardware projects and a senior editor at *Make* magazine, for anyone who created and released free software allowing Kinect to work with any computer rather than just the Xbox. Once that happens, watch out, application developers will go to town prototyping and testing new ways to leverage the capability. It's only a matter of time before we see new gesture-based applications and platforms. How about gesture-based health care and education applications to start?

Of course, Microsoft's reaction to all of this was interesting. Their initial knee-jerk reaction was, as expected, negative. Initially the company was caught flat-footed, saying it didn't condone product tampering and threatened legal action against hackers. Think, Apple. However, I have to give Microsoft some credit; once market enthusiasm for Kinect became clear and sales started taking off with 2.5 million of the motion sensors sold within the first month after launch, the company began to get open innovation religion. Okay, maybe that's an exaggeration, but Microsoft stopped threatening hackers with legal action and at least publicly embraced hacker enthusiasm to explore new uses for Kinect. Maybe there is hope that Microsoft can be cool again! Hacking capabilities can unleash new sources of value and solutions for many of the social system challenges we face today. We should encourage capability hackers and make it easier for them to work their magic. We need to try more stuff. Innovators, hack away. Experiment all the time.

Principle 13. Off the Whiteboard and into the Real World

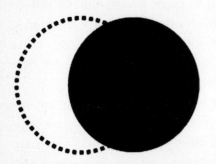

Move quickly from the theoretical to the actual. Real-world change has more variables than you can anticipate. Experimentation yields rich results.

It is easy to sketch out business model innovation scenarios on the whiteboard. It is far more difficult to take the idea off the whiteboard for a spin in the real world. We need safe and manageable platforms for real-world experimentation of new business models and social systems. Since most leaders in the twenty-first century will likely have to change their business models several times over their careers it makes sense to do R&D for new business models the same way R&D is done for new products and technologies today. Create the space for exploration. We need to create the conditions in the real world for ongoing experimentation of new business models and social systems.

If organizations of all kinds need to experiment with new business models in the real world and communities need to become more relevant in order to strengthen their local economies, here's an idea: Why not turn cities into innovation hot spots or platforms to enable ongoing experimentation of new business models and social systems? It would create the conditions for public and private sector organizations to continually explore new business models, while at the same time helping communities access new solutions and a stronger local economy for its citizens. Sounds like a win-win scenario to me.

In 2010 I participated in an Economic Development Roundtable in Detroit providing a perfect forum to float the idea. Before going to the event, participants were asked to answer the following question:

> Given your experience, what are the most "game-changing" ways to use a significant amount of grant funding ($100 million+) to change the trajectory of an urban economy? In other words, if you were given a free hand to use $100 million+ of grants, what would you do?

Here is how I answered: I suggest that we turn cities into innovation hotspots. We need a new national economic development conversation. It should bubble up from cities. We are playing defense based on old industrial economy rules and systems. We must play offense to create a twenty-first century innovation economy that all citizens can fully participate in. An innovation economy will provide citizens with a viable job ladder and good higher wage job opportunities. It will also enable solutions for the big system challenges we face including health care, education, workforce development, and energy sustainability. These are system challenges that will not be fixed with incremental tweaks. We must design, demonstrate, and deploy new system approaches to these challenges. The solutions should be coming from our cities. Cities should be living labs. If cities become innovation hot spots, new investment and jobs will be created. We need ongoing R&D for new transformative models and systems. Developing a twenty-first century innovation economy depends on it.

The good news is that given the scope of economic challenges our cities face, there is more receptivity to innovation than ever. Cities offer a perfect nexus and can catalyze economic transformation. Cities are comprised of emergent networks with the assets necessary to become innovation hotspots. We should help turn a targeted group of cities into innovation hotspots to serve as national and global models for economic transformation. They can demonstrate to the nation and to the world that all citizens can participate in an innovation economy and become active R&D labs for solution development on the big system challenges of our day.

If I could deploy $100 million (not nearly enough but a good start), I would launch "Cities as Innovation Hotspots." Cities would compete to be selected to become partners in a national program to create replicable models and tools to strengthen the innovation capacity of our nation's urban centers and actionable platforms for ongoing system solution development in areas of high social importance and impact. Too much of our current effort is incremental and fragmented. Too much government and foundation investment is spread thin among the usual suspects and is going toward point solutions that will only serve to sustain our current systems. We are not investing in platforms that can make necessary disruptive change better understood and safer to scale. Sustaining investments would be fine if the current systems we live and operate in could be improved to transform our economy and social systems. It is not possible. We need to learn how to design and explore new systems while pedaling the bicycle of our current systems. We need safe and manageable environments to experiment at the systems level. Let's identify cities with the necessary public and private sector leadership, institutional capacity for change, and a motivated community to make the local commitment necessary to serve as national examples for the required transformation.

We don't have to invent anything new. The silos and systems we are stuck in have evolved over a long period of time. They are well-intentioned but not capable of disrupting themselves to take advantage of new technologies to enable new solutions and better value for citizens, consumers, students, and patients. We need new systems and a path to demonstrate that new models and approaches work in the real world and can scale. We have to create the environment and platforms that can enable business model and systems-level experimentation and change.

Cities as Innovation Hot Spots would be a catalyst for change and a real-world lab to advance new business model and system solutions. Cities would be selected and connected in a network to leverage a common framework for measuring and increasing innovation capacity. Each city would share a common framework for defining economic development objectives and measuring progress. Each city would target specific focus areas (health care, education, energy, transportation, housing, workforce development, etc.) for system design and experimentation in the real-world lab of their city. An Innovation Story Studio would be shared across selected cities to package and share the stories of progress in order to create an emotional connection and strong grass-roots engagement both within and across target cities.

I went to Detroit to pitch the idea and got a big wake-up call. It was the first time I had visited Detroit. Talk about a burning platform. If you need a call to action just visit Detroit and see the devastation for yourself. This once great industrial city is a shell of its former self. Detroit has lost half of its population, going from a peak in the 1950s of 2 million to under 1 million in the 2000 Census. It is expected that the population will settle below 700,000 as unemployment and home foreclosures continue to fuel out-migration. What is to become of those that can't get out and are left behind?

Real unemployment rates in Detroit are thought to be as high as 50 percent and block-by-block surveys indicate that about one in three land parcels are either vacant or abandoned. Arne Duncan, Secretary of Education, called Detroit Public Schools a national disgrace that keeps him up at night. The current mayor, Dave Bing, is talking about downsizing the city, including drastic plans to relocate residents from desolate to stable neighborhoods.

You get the picture. It is enough to make you cry. Detroit isn't the only urban center that has been devastated by the departure of an industrial era along with its good manufacturing jobs. Is your city far behind Detroit? The need for bold moves and real systems change seems so obvious. We can't possibly address these challenges with tweaks to our current economic, education, and workforce development systems.

I went to Detroit hoping for a transformative conversation about changing the trajectory of our urban economies. I had high expectations, but the well-intentioned leaders assembled seemed resigned to working within current economic development models and systems to change our urban outcomes. I guess I naively expected more outrage and a greater sense of urgency for bold action to change the trajectory.

Maybe I am too impatient and biased on the need for disruptive innovation, but I can't help hoping that burning platforms like Detroit will light a fire to enable bolder thinking and action. After listening for a while I asserted that if we want to change the trajectory of urban economies we should start by changing the trajectory of our conversation. There was little traction for the premise that we need to or can transform industrial-era systems that have evolved over a long period of time and seem unchangeable. Note to self: I need to get much better and clearer at articulating the imperative for R&D at the systems level.

After having led the economic development effort in Rhode Island it was like déjà vu for me to participate in an economic development conversation with the main thrust being how to attract more venture capital, advance cluster strategies, scale entrepreneurial support programs, and get economic and workforce development programs to actually talk with one another. Not that these programs aren't necessary and important but anyone who thinks we are going to turn around Detroit or any other urban center without disruptive system change is kidding themselves.

The system change we need must be directly relevant to real people in real neighborhoods. Citizens living at and below national poverty levels in our urban centers are so far removed from talk about venture capital and an innovation economy it isn't funny. We need to transform our economic, education, and workforce development systems now. They must be designed around the citizen and not around institutions with a vested interest in today's systems. We need to demonstrate that a new system approach is directly relevant to citizens at every wage, experience, and education level. Every citizen in every neighborhood must see an accessible job ladder and feasible path forward. Every citizen, not just those of us with access to better economic and education opportunities, must believe and see how they can participate in an innovation economy.

We need to design, explore, and scale new business models and systems around the citizen with direct connections at the neighborhood level. Our rhetoric is too much about institutions and not enough about real people. We are too focused on current systems and not bold enough to design and experiment with new system approaches. What are we waiting for? Let's turn our cities into innovation hotspots and living laboratories. Our citizens are waiting. Cities as innovation labs would be perfect platforms to enable all organizations to do ongoing R&D for new business models in the real world.

Principle 14. It's a User-centered World— Design for It

Insight starts with empathy. Center yourself around the voice and experience of the end-user. Put it at the heart of the innovation process. Your products and services will be forever relevant.

The imperative of our time is to unleash the power of business model innovation. I think a lot about how to simplify the business model innovation narrative, make it more inclusive, and become more experimental. Unleashing the power of business model innovation is about making customer experience central, focusing on outputs and looking up from our silos.

For starters, we need a shared definition for business model innovation. Our rhetoric is all over the place and innovation has become a buzzword. Everything is an innovation and everyone is an innovator. When that happens, nothing and no one is. We conflate invention with innovation. They are not the same. A simple definition: Business model innovation is a better way to create, deliver, and capture value. It is not innovation until value is delivered one customer at a time. Often we don't have to invent anything new to deliver value or solve a problem. We have to get better at reconfiguring and combining existing capabilities to deliver value. It is not technology that is preventing business model innovation. It is stubborn humans and organizations that resist change.

I am amazed at the number of innovation discussions where the voice of the end-user is missing. Customer experience must be at the heart of any innovation and design process. Solutions are not about institutions organized to deliver them, they are about consumers, patients, students, and citizens.

Far too much attention and resources are focused on the inputs versus the outputs of innovation. There are more ideas and new technologies than we could ever use or implement. There are too many inventions stuck in the garage or lab. We need to get more ideas and solutions off of the whiteboard and into the real world. The imperative is more real-world experimentation. We need to try more stuff to see what works and is scalable. If you are like me, it drives you crazy when one branch of government has no idea about your interaction with the department right next door, and when one part of the health-care system can't seem to share information or collaborate with any other part. Don't get me started on education. It just makes me cry.

We have the inputs for business model innovation at our disposal. Our focus needs to shift to the outputs. It isn't an innovation until value is delivered. Innovation should be measured based on outcomes. Are there proof points that the solution works in the real world and at scale? We need to invest in platforms and tools to enable new model and system experiments. We need to organize safe zones where we can try new approaches in the real world designed around the end-user. We are in love with inputs. We have bought in to the invention narrative and haven't been successful at replacing it with a compelling innovation story. Making progress on the social challenges of our time also requires us to stop hunkering down in our silos. Excessive introspection and self-absorption will not enable system-level solutions.

We need to collaborate with unusual suspects across organizations, disciplines, and sectors. System-level challenges like health care, education, and energy require system-level experimentation and innovation. We have to make collaboration a natural act. It will only happen if we lean against the human tendency to stay in our silos, and we move beyond comfortable solutions that are within our sphere of influence. The imperative is to enable collaborative innovation. We can design and scale new systems that take advantage of twenty-first century technology if we move beyond our normal tendency to stay entrenched within comfortable silos.

We are fortunate to live in an exciting time where big things are possible. It is the innovator's day. We don't have to invent anything new. Unleashing the power of innovation is about making customer experience central, focusing on outputs, and looking up from our silos.

Principle 15. A Decade Is a Terrible Thing to Waste

Commit to transformational change. Hold yourselves accountable for making headway. There is real urgency: 87,600 hours to go. What are we waiting for?

It's the innovator's day, but we have to act now with a sense of urgency. If you are reading this book you are a like-minded innovation junkie. It's a good place to be right now because there's no more important time for all of us to fulfill our potential as innovators. We have the capacity to lead the way out of this economic mess and toward solutions for the big issues of our time. We must play offense.

Here's some good news: Innovators thrive during turbulent times. The bad news is that innovation has become a buzzword. Everything is an innovation and everyone is an innovation expert. We must get below the buzzwords. I have a simple definition: Innovation is a better way to deliver value. I also differentiate invention from innovation. I assert it is not an innovation until it delivers real value to a consumer.

Ideas, inventions, and new technologies are the lifeblood for innovation. We must continue to invest in basic and discovery research. It is necessary, but it is not sufficient. We also must improve our ability to get inventions out of the lab and into the real world, where they can solve problems and deliver value. Business model innovation is the key to realizing the full potential of new technologies. A business model is a network of capabilities and a sustainable financial model to deliver value to target customers. Successful executives are really good at squeezing more value from existing business models. In this context, innovation means either revenue growth from new products and services or reducing operating costs with process improvements. For most, innovation is about finding ways to ring the cash register by pedaling the bicycle of today's business model faster.

While there's nothing wrong with an incremental strategy, there is a problem. Business models aren't lasting as long as they used to, and most CEOs have only had to lead a single business model throughout their career. Going forward, I suspect CEOs will have to change business models several times over a career and establish an ongoing process to explore new business models—even models that might threaten the current one. Organizations must establish R&D for new business models the way they do R&D for new products and services today. Business model innovation needs a discrete focus or it will get marginalized, producing again only incremental change.

In today's networked world, business model innovation means connecting capabilities across traditional boundaries. Companies, schools, and government agencies all must rethink existing business models and all struggle with the capacity to explore and test new ways to deliver value. Don't you wonder, as I do, with so much new technology available why we haven't made more progress? Technology isn't the barrier to business model innovation. It is our stubborn resistance to experimentation and change. Everyone loves the idea of innovation, until it has a personal impact. I used to think that we could enable large-scale change and create more innovators by proselytizing. But that doesn't get you past the buzzwords. I now believe in sorting the world to identify the innovators and finding ways to connect them in purposeful ways.

The best opportunities to create value will be found in the gray areas between silos, sectors, and disciplines. And progress on the big-system issues of our time will require a road map and manageable platforms for business model and systems-level experimentation and change. It doesn't matter if the customer is a patient, student, citizen, or consumer. R&D for new business models is imperative to remain competitive, harness technology, and deliver more value with fewer resources.

We need a greater sense of urgency to enable market making versus share taking. Business model innovators are market makers. Are you a market maker or a share taker? I find that most of the world is made up of share takers. Share takers focus on getting a bigger slice of an existing pie. It is understandable. It is easier to find a market that is already defined with the competitive rules of the road clearly marked and competitors easily identified. It is far more difficult to create a new pie. New markets without established competitive rules and competitors are uncharted territory. There are far fewer market makers. Yet making new markets is more exciting than working hard to get and keep a share point in a market defined by others. The biggest value creation opportunities belong to the market makers. We learn more from market makers and they tend to be passionate people and companies we want to be connected to. Wanted: market makers.

The problem with being a share taker is that someone else has defined the market and all you can do is compete for a part of it. If you open a local shoe store you will compete with other shoe stores in your area. Your inventory of shoes will look similar and you will probably compete on friendly service and a convenient location. If the shoe store down the road has a sale you will probably have a sale too, to stay competitive. You will live the life of a share taker, pedaling very hard to maintain business and to grow by enticing customers from the shoe store down the street. Meet Tony Hsieh, the CEO of Zappos. If you ask Tony he will tell you that they are not in the shoe business, although that is what Zappos is most known for today. Tony says that Zappos is in the online customer service business, and while shoes are the biggest part of their business today, they may not be in the future. Zappos is a market maker. They are defining the standard of customer service for online sales. Zappos does not see the local shoe store as the competition and I bet that the local shoe store would say that they are not competing with Zappos.

The year 2008 was the 10-year anniversary of the MP3 player. Over 70 digital music players have been introduced over the 10-year history of the market. All of the share takers trying to capture share in a market defined as MP3 players are either gone or pale in comparison to the market for digital music that Apple has created and leads with the iPod and iTunes. It is a classic market maker story. The music player is just an enabler within an ecosystem that allows the consumer to easily carry personal digital music collections with them wherever they go. Apple created a system around the enabling technology and never defined the market as the MP3 market. Rather than settling for a share of the existing MP3 market in October of 2001 when the first iPod was introduced, Apple set out to create and lead the digital music market. Once Apple's iPod, the market maker, took off, the share takers were left to respond. Apple has never looked back and the iPod and iTunes story is one of the best examples of the difference between market making and share taking.

Market makers define the rules. They set the pricing in their markets and have more growth potential than share takers. If you are a market maker you know that you can't rest on your laurels. Market making is an ongoing process. As soon as you establish a new market, share takers immediately come after it. If you don't continue to be a market maker you will find that you can quickly start to behave like a share taker in protecting the market you originally created. Don't let it happen. Continue to look for ways to be a market maker. Market makers create more value and have more fun in the process. Wanted: market makers with a sense of urgency, because a decade is a terrible thing to waste.

Creating a Business Model Innovation Factory

7 R&D for New Business Models

I f only we could have started the twenty-first century by putting up a "closed for renovation" sign, clearing the way to transform our current business models and industry structures. We don't have the luxury. Business models don't last as long as they used to. Tweaks won't work and nothing short of business model innovation and industry transformation is needed. Our collective challenge is to catalyze transformational change while continuing to pedal the bicycle of today's business models. We need real-world platforms, connected to existing business models, with the autonomy and resources to design, prototype, and experiment with transformational solutions. Going to war with current business models won't work. If we're going to transform anything we should start by putting up an "open for renovation" sign.

Have you ever done a major renovation of your home while you were still living in it? We did. I don't know what we were thinking. I'm not talking about a tweak. It's the familiar story about a project that started off as a manageable kitchen remodeling. Then the "while we're at it we might as well do this too" started. Before the dust finally settled, 75 percent of the living space in our home was transformed, all while we continued to live in the house. Talk about disruption! Like all transformations, it took twice as long and cost twice as much as predicted.

If you ask our three children, who had to live through it, I'm sure each would say they were scarred for life by the trauma. For two years we were nomads in our own home, with sleeping arrangements changing constantly. It was an adventure to find the temporary kitchen location on any given day. Tweaking is easy. Transformation isn't. No wonder our current business models are so resistant to transformational change.

In the end our house came out great and we were thrilled with the result, but looking back we would've been better off if we had found an alternative temporary living arrangement. We don't have the luxury of putting up a "closed for renovation" sign while we transform our social systems. We have to get better at experimenting with new business models while still living in the current ones. Big bang approaches to organization or system change seldom work. Instead of going to war to transform an entrenched business model, create real-world sandboxes right next door in which a new generation of transformative business models can be explored. To enable transformative change consider creating connected adjacencies as innovation platforms.

The imperative is to do R&D for new business models the way organizations do R&D for new products and technologies today. The trick is to explore and test new business models while at the same time continuing to live within current ones. This requires establishing adjacent innovation platforms with the freedom to explore new ways to create and deliver value, especially approaches that are disruptive to the current model. Adjacent innovation platforms must have the freedom to experiment with different rules and financial models. Connected adjacencies require senior leadership sponsorship, support, and protection or they will fail. They must be free to recombine and connect capabilities in new ways, unconstrained by the existing organization. Those working in the adjacencies must be empowered to borrow and flexibly deploy capabilities and technologies from inside and outside the organization in novel ways.

Innovate through Connected Adjacencies

Don't go to war with current business models. Too many are in love with them and you will lose. Create the future through connected adjacencies. Why are innovators so quick to go to the mattresses? Like a scene right out of *The Godfather*, innovators are wired to assume a war footing. Innovators start from a premise that intransigent business models and industry structures are the enemy and the only way to win is to gear up for an inevitable fight. Status quo is the enemy in an innovator's cold war and must be vanquished. Innovators prepare for war by steeling themselves, building large armamentariums, and recruiting passionate soldiers to join their fight. War cries may get people's attention but taking to the warpath as a theory for change doesn't work. There are too many people in love with their current business models. Going to war might feel good, but in the end you will lose.

Existing business models and industry structures have evolved over a long period of time. It's true most were built for an industrial era that is long gone. It's also true all organizations need to design, prototype, and test new business models. However, going to war with current business models will not work. Too many people are vested in them. Anything threatening status quo is too scary to contemplate for most. Big bang approaches to change seldom work. Occasionally we see examples of organizations that disrupt and transform themselves because they are either one payroll away from crashing nose down into the K-Mart parking lot (IBM comes to mind), or they have an otherworldly leader that personally wills the organization to transform (Steve Jobs comes to mind). For most organizations transformative change is elusive and we need another way. To enable transformative change, consider creating connected adjacencies as innovation platforms.

Here's how the idea works. Instead of going to war to transform an entrenched business model, create real-world sandboxes right next door in which a new generation of transformative business models can be explored. The imperative is to do R&D for new business models the way organizations do R&D for new products and technologies today. The trick is to explore and test new models, while at the same time continuing to operate within the current model. This requires establishing adjacent innovation platforms with the freedom to explore new ways to create, deliver, and capture value, including approaches that are disruptive to the current model. Adjacent innovation platforms must have the freedom to experiment with different rules and financial models.

The idea of enabling business model innovation through connected adjacencies borrows from an insightful concept developed by the scientist Stuart Kaufman, who first described the untapped potential of what could be as the "adjacent possible." Kaufman's concept is that innovation is merely the recombination of existing parts assembled in new ways to solve a problem or deliver value. Everything we need to innovate can be found in the adjacent spaces right next to us if we just allow ourselves to climb to the edge of our current organizations and perspectives. Innovation is all about exploring the adjacent possible.

Author Stephen Johnson describes the underlying idea behind connected adjacencies well: "Ideas are works of bricolage. They are, almost inevitably, networks of other ideas. We take the ideas we've inherited or stumbled across, and we jigger them together into some new shape. The adjacent possible is a kind of shadow future, hovering on the edges of the present state of things, a map of all the ways in which the present can reinvent itself.

The strange and beautiful truth about the adjacent possible is that its boundaries grow as you explore them. Each new combination opens up the possibility of other new combinations."[1]

Think about it. Doesn't all evolution work that way? Life evolved out of the primordial soup by recombining what already existed and taking advantage of the adjacent possible. Random collisions create

---

[1] "The Genius of the Tinkerer," *Wall Street Journal*, September 25, 2010.

new first-order combinations. More collisions enable second-order combinations and before you know it there are seven billion of us inhabiting the planet. Cultural innovation follows the same evolutionary path, taking advantage of the adjacent possible. Guttenberg converted wine press technology into the printing press. Vacuum tubes became integrated circuits. Everything is a result of leveraging what already existed. Innovation isn't about coming up with the next big idea, it is about recombining existing ideas and parts in new ways. It is about leveraging the building blocks that create the space of what is possible. Too many think innovation is about getting more new ideas on the table. It is about getting more building blocks on the table and learning how to combine and recombine them in exciting new ways.

Business model innovation works the same way. Think of capabilities or the power to do something as the building blocks. Business model innovation is really just learning how to combine and recombine capabilities in new ways to deliver value. Creating a connected adjacency or sandbox to freely play with new combinations is the best way to design, prototype, and test new business models.

Connected adjacencies require senior leadership sponsorship, support, and protection or they will fail. They must be free to recombine and connect capabilities in new ways, unconstrained by the existing organization. Those working in the adjacencies must be empowered to borrow and flexibly deploy capabilities and technologies from inside and outside the organization in novel ways.

Innovation sandboxes must be connected to existing business models. Transparent and open connections enable a two-way exchange of ideas and experience. Connections allow inhabitants of current models to self-select to play in designing new ones. Don't force anyone to participate. Make involvement and assignments to play in the innovation sandbox optional. It's amazing how innovators will migrate to adjacent platforms. They won't want to be left out. Some will dive in and play in committed ways while others will want to dip their toes in the water while keeping feet firmly planted in the current model. Encourage the flow. If we expose more people to business model experiments and demonstrate feasibility in the real world, change may seem more accessible and less scary. If we stand up new business models in safe adjacent spaces, more will willingly make the leap.

My friend and Babson College president Len Schlesinger is the master of leveraging connected adjacencies. When he became Babson's president, Len inherited an institution founded in 1919 with a proud and long-standing tradition. Like most colleges, Babson has a well-accepted set of operating rules and norms that define how the place works. It's been working pretty well, as Babson is perennially ranked number one in the world for teaching entrepreneurship. And yet Schlesinger and his leadership team know that higher education must change and Babson is no exception. He also knows that going to war with the current Babson business model and its 325 acres, entrenched infrastructure, bricks and mortar, and 170 faculty members with lifetime employment is a bad strategy that won't work. Instead, Len and the Babson team work on creating the future through connected adjacencies.

At Schlesinger's direction and with his support Babson has created Babson Global, a separate entity adjacent to Babson's core business model, to serve as an R&D platform enabling the design, prototyping, and testing of new approaches to making entrepreneurship central to our global economic future. The connected adjacency has the autonomy to experiment with new models for both teaching entrepreneurship and creating entrepreneurial ecosystems in communities around the world. At the same time the platform is transparent and welcomes ideas and participation from faculty and staff from across the college. The one thing that Schlesinger's constant attention to the platform ensures is that stakeholders in the core business model are not allowed to block or prevent the development and exploration of new approaches, even those that may seem threatening to the core model.

Our team at BIF has been working closely with Schlesinger and Babson to help stand up their connected adjacency. Within Babson Global we are enabling R&D for new business models by creating a real-world laboratory called the Entrepreneur Experience Lab. Together we are creating a real-world innovation platform to explore and test new entrepreneur support solutions and models. We are just getting started, but I can already see the strategy of connected adjacencies working as Babson leaders and faculty self-select to play. It's a powerful approach.

Len Schlesinger has it exactly right when he says that we need to move from thinking our way into action to acting our way into thinking. By creating a business model innovation platform as a connected adjacency to Babson's core model he is creating the conditions for business model experimentation by balancing the need for autonomy with the need for access and connectivity with the current business model.

I first became interested in business model experimentation during my road warrior consulting days. While a partner at Accenture from 1992 to 2002, client after client would comment on the ease with which we assembled and reassembled consulting teams based on the specific customer need we were addressing. Our teams would come together seamlessly from across geographic offices and skill areas to work collaboratively on whatever project they were assigned to. It was completely transparent what part of the Accenture organization each individual came from. All that mattered was solving the client's need. When the project was completed individuals were then redeployed to the next challenge, often collaborating with an entirely new group of team members. Over the years senior client executives would often lament to me that they would kill to be able to deploy and redeploy employees from across functions, geography, and business units as seamlessly as we did to a steady flow of project assignments.

In example after example I found companies constrained by organization structures making it extremely difficult to temporarily deploy employees to projects requiring skills and experience from multiple functions across the company. Functional boundaries were impermeable, making it extremely difficult to implement cross-functional processes and almost impossible to experiment with new approaches. Executives I worked with over the years knew that more flexible organizational approaches were needed, but were incapable of moving away from the rigid functional structures. I saw and helped construct many workarounds to try and increase the effectiveness of cross-functional teams, but the main allegiance of those deployed was always back to their home functions where career and salary advancement decisions were controlled.

It wasn't just the capacity at Accenture to continually deploy and redeploy teams from across our organization that impressed executives. It was also the way we changed our entire business model seemingly at will. Over the 10 years I was a partner in the firm we completely reorganized at least four times. Change became a way of life and came to be expected throughout the organization. Client executives couldn't believe a company the size of Accenture with over 230,000 employees, operations in 120 countries, and revenues of over $25 billion could reorganize from top to bottom so seamlessly and quickly.

Even more amazing to many is the fact that Accenture operates without a formal headquarters. Imagine any organization of that size and scale without a headquarters where all the senior executives reside. Accenture's senior executive team is spread out around the world, connected by clear management processes with each executive's role being well-defined. When the CEO or any senior management position opens up or changes hands the individual named to the position doesn't move to a central headquarters but assumes the assigned role seamlessly from the office location they reside in.

I participated in and saw firsthand several huge business model changes that I'm certain none of our clients could have pulled off because of our flexible leadership and operating model. The first big transition was when Accenture changed its business model from being a system integrator to being a business integrator. The firm's value proposition went from making the deployment of large-scale information and transaction systems predictable to making large-scale business systems predictable. Accenture had become the premiere systems integrator in the market but knew that to create sustainable business value required the integration of a business strategy with people, process, and technology. The firm was loaded with skills and experience on the technology side but to become a premier business integrator it needed to add strategy, process design, and change management capabilities. The challenge faced by the firm was how to build new capabilities requiring entirely different skills and experiences when everything about the existing business model was about being a great systems integrator. At the time the partners in the firm had all grown up with the firm and were all promoted from within. It was a proud and successful culture of partners and professionals moving up the partner track who had built an incredible market leadership position in the systems integration market. But to transform the firm's business model to create and lead an entirely new market called business integration would require a connected adjacency to allow for the establishment of new business model components while simultaneously continuing to operate within the existing one.

I joined Accenture (Andersen Consulting at the time) as a partner in 1992 as part of an effort to rapidly build a strategy capability alongside the existing system integration business. It was a connected adjacency given the autonomy and resources necessary to scale a rapidly growing strategy practice from scratch right next to the huge systems integration practice. We were an entrepreneurial business unit within the context of the behemoth. The emergent strategy practice would never have worked if it had to live by the rules of the core business model at the time. If not protected it would have been swallowed alive by line partners from within the core business model. The new business model needed to be shielded, at least temporarily, within the relative safety of a connected adjacency.

For starters, it was unheard of within the firm to hire direct admit partners who hadn't paid their dues growing up within the firm. In order to accelerate the establishment of a premiere strategy practice within Accenture, it was essential. Almost everything about the new practice was different than the core business model, ranging from salary structure, to titles, to how projects were priced, to how projects were staffed and how they were done. Senior management knew that the only way to achieve its business integration vision was to provide the strategy practice with the autonomy to create the model that made sense in order to scale it successfully.

They also knew it was essential that it remain connected to the core business to leverage infrastructure, to make sure that activities could be coordinated at common clients, and most importantly, to ensure that once the strategy practice had reached sufficient scale it could be integrated with the core systems integration practice into the new business integration model, which was the key growth driver of the firm over the next 10 years. There were organizational conflicts all along the way that had to be worked out but the business model innovation approach worked beautifully, enabling the creation first of a strategy practice, which represented a completely new business model in of itself, and then ultimately the creation of an even more powerful new business model that integrated multiple service lines to deliver on Accenture's business integration proposition.

As if that wasn't enough of a major business change to live through, I also participated in other changes that were equally transformational in the 10 years I was at Accenture. When I joined the firm in 1992 we went to market by geography. Everything at the time was organized by region and office. There was a managing partner for each office and everyone in the office reported to him or her. The office had responsibility for serving clients within the geography assigned to the office. It worked well and the firm grew rapidly while executing a business model focused on delivering general system integration services.

A couple of signals emerged, suggesting that Accenture's existing business model could be threatened. First, as the dollars invested in large-scale information and transactional systems skyrocketed, more and more executives were beginning to question the business value of making such large investments. They were asking for clearer business cases before making big IT system investments. The market was demanding that IT and business strategy be better aligned. Secondly, competitors were emerging to go after the attractive systems integration business. Companies had more choices to select from when hiring a systems integration firm and, predictably, downward price pressure was being applied in the market. The margins were still very attractive and Accenture had a significant leadership position, but there were clear warning signs on the horizon. We could either ignore the signals, continuing to exclusively focus on expanding and protecting the systems integration business model, or we could reinvent our business model to change the way value was created, delivered, and captured. Accenture chose the latter path, wanting to create and lead an entirely new business and market model.

But in order to deliver value in the firm's new business integration model it had to deliver deep industry skills and experience to ensure information and transaction systems were aligned with business strategies. It didn't make sense and wasn't feasible to develop deep industry skills in every office, while it had been possible to ensure that every office had general systems integration skills while working in the old business model.

When it became important to deploy industry skills and experience to the point of need wherever the client was located, Accenture at first experimented with a new business model that was organized around industry sector rather than geography and then fully changed its business model to go to market by industry. Instead of having a managing partner for every office, leadership was deployed to run the business by industry. It turned the entire way the firm operated on its head, changing the way the business model created, delivered, and captured value. The entire firm transitioned to the new business model, including the reassignment of the majority of the people within the firm. Consultants across service lines were assigned to industry operating units that spanned offices across geography. There was no longer a managing partner assigned to each office location. It was a huge cultural change for the firm and everyone in it. It was a change that few, if any, of my clients at the time could have managed to pull off.

The new business model was tried first within regions then rolled out nationally and ultimately globally. It was amazing how seamlessly a company the size of Accenture handled the transition. Not without stress and transition conflict but relatively smoothly compared to the difficulty that many of my clients had making business model shifts that were nowhere near as transformational as the ones I lived through while at Accenture. While these business model changes were going on at Accenture the one thing that never changed was a religious focus on serving the client. Once anyone from anywhere in the firm was assigned to a client project that was the only thing that mattered. The entire organization could be changing around the team and they would stay focused on making sure that the project went well. Client service was the North Star and routinely changing the organization was expected and welcome as long as we all believed the firm would continue to get stronger and grow. We had evidence from living through multiple re-organizations that while stressful in the short term, changing made us all more relevant in the market and better able to deploy the necessary skills to solve a client's need.

Another major business model shift that was still ongoing after I left Accenture in 2002 was a transition from a financial model that was solely fee-for-service to one driven by long-term outsourcing contracts. Instead of getting paid based on the time spent by consulting staff to deliver against a specific project objective multiplied by the billing rates of the staff assigned, a growing percentage of the firm's income came from contracts to not only design and build new capabilities but also to operate them on behalf of the client. Many clients liked this kind of arrangement because it shifted the risk that a new system would work as designed to the company providing the outsourcing service and it allowed clients to keep their internal headcount down as the new capabilities are operated by staff employed by the outsourcer. Offering what we called Business Process Outsourcing, or BPO services, opened up new sources of long-term revenue and again changed the basis of competition, making it difficult for other consulting firms without a BPO offering to compete for the lucrative capability design and build work.

Just like creating a new strategy practice at Accenture required a connected adjacency to the core business in order to develop and scale the necessary capabilities for a different business model, so did establishing a successful BPO business model. Everything about the BPO business was different than the core Accenture business model. If we had applied the same pricing and profitability model from the core consulting business to the BPO business it would never have worked. If we deployed consultants at the same billing rates and tried to recover overhead at the same rates as the core consulting business, we would never have been able to grow a successful BPO business. It required experimentation and tolerance for mistakes. And boy, there were some doozies.

When a mistake is made in pricing a large outsourcing contract it really hurts and is difficult to recover from. By setting the business up as a separate unit or connected adjacency with strong senior management support, over time mistakes became fewer and the new business model began to take hold and ultimately became a big contributor to Accenture's business success and growth. The new business model required completely different leadership, skills, operating practices, and procedures. If these BPO opportunities had been subjected to the same rules as the core business they would have never been pursued, and if any made it through the cracks the emerging business model would have been shut down after the first large costly mistake.

Providing sourcing services for core and infrastructure capabilities and temporary access to staff to fill short-term human resource needs has become a huge business. In difficult economic times like the current downturn facing all organizations, the risk of adding full-time employees to the payroll is being avoided with gaps filled by staffing and outsourcing services. In fact, if you look at the Inc. 5000 list of the fastest growing companies in the United States over the last five years and examine the top 10 job creators over that period, all of them are staffing companies. Work has become project-based and variable.

The BPO example both demonstrates how new business models only thrive when provided with the conditions to experiment with new capability combinations unconstrained by the existing business model, but also indicates an important trend for all business model innovators. Capabilities no longer need to be locked into rigid organization structures. They can be combined and recombined in new and exciting ways. Capabilities can be sourced from multiple organizations and networked together to explore and scale new business models. The key to business model innovation is the ability to play with the parts in flexible ways to create new value. Capabilities just want to be free! Being locked into rigid organization structures gets in the way of business model innovation.

If you lead a product company you are probably saying, sure Accenture is a service company making it easier to change. While it may be easier for a service organization than a product manufacturing company to rearrange capabilities in new configurations to change its business model, I found over the years that both have extreme difficulty changing the way their business models work. Rigid organizational structures and cultures that are not wired for constant change constrain all organizations. There are many service organizations—hospitals and colleges come to mind—that are just as stuck in their current business models and vulnerable to disruption as any industrial-era manufacturing company. The opposite is also true with many product companies—Apple and IBM come to mind—that are fantastic examples of transformational business model change. Successful business model innovators are always exploring their next business model while they continue to operate with the current one, before it is too late to change. R&D for new business models is the new strategic imperative.

8 Leading and Organizing a Business Model Innovation Factory

The first step in creating a business model innovation factory is an explicit leadership decision to explore and test new business models. It may seem basic and obvious, but without establishing a clear and discreet business model innovation objective at the very top of the organization, it won't happen. Business model innovation must be led from the top. It won't happen bottom up. It won't happen through well-intentioned efforts by midlevel managers with a passion for innovation. It won't happen by creating a culture of innovation throughout the organization focused on strengthening the current business model. Business model innovation requires the capacity to act outside of the interests of the current business model. It will only happen with the sponsorship and support of the CEO and requires a dedicated and focused effort that is protected from those in the current business model that want to block or waylay any new business model that is distracting or disruptive.

Leading and organizing a business model innovation factory is different than creating an innovation platform or lab to support the current business model. Establishing innovation as a strategic management imperative and creating an innovation department accountable to line management isn't good enough if you want to design, prototype, and test new business models. It may be good enough to strengthen your current business model. Creating an innovation department accountable to line management should produce new product and service revenue opportunities, open up new customer markets, and increase operating efficiencies, but it will not result in new business models. It is important to distinguish between the two objectives.

Most companies I visit have established innovation as an organizational strategic objective and many have even created a department or function to achieve it. Innovation has become the latest management buzzword and I have found companies all over the map in their capacity to get below the buzzwords to deliver real value to the organization. Many corporate innovation leaders are tasked with the vague objective of creating an innovation culture throughout the organization and the more specific objective of helping business units and line executives improve the top-line performance and operating efficiency of the company. In my experience corporate innovation departments, despite any rhetoric suggesting bolder business model innovation objectives, are primarily focused on creating and implementing an innovation agenda that will improve the performance of the existing business model.

I have heard countless senior executives give speeches to their organizations claiming that innovation is the only way to stay competitive. The speeches always go on to implore everyone in the organization to think "out of the box" and to act more boldly. But when the speeches are over and senior management goes back to the top floor and plush carpets, all of the innovation rhetoric gets refocused on ideas and initiatives that map directly back to the current business model. Line executives ask, how do we find new revenue opportunities that can be exploited through our current go-to-market model and that meet the return threshold of our current financial model? They also ask, how do we strengthen our current capabilities to more efficiently create, deliver, and capture value from our current business model? When is the last time you heard a line executive ask, is there a new and better business model we should explore even if it is distracting and disruptive to our current one?

There must be a discreet objective in any corporate innovation agenda for business model innovation or it will not happen. There must be a clear mandate from the top to explore and test new business models. It can't be conflated with a broad innovation mandate that also includes improvements to the current business model. If the responsibility to oversee, fund, staff, and select innovation projects is with line management, guess which projects will be selected? Creating an innovation department accountable to line management with responsibility to operate today's business model is necessary but not sufficient if the objective is to explore and test new business models. A separate platform accountable outside of line management is required for business model innovation.

A business model innovation factory must be a separate activity designed as a connected adjacency with its own leadership, staff, resources, and reporting relationship accountable to the CEO. It should also have the blessing and support of the board of directors. The examples of Blockbuster and Apple demonstrate the importance of support from the top, including the board, to enable business model innovation. In the case of Blockbuster, when John Antioco was the chairman and CEO and wanted to move the company toward a new online business model, he was ultimately thwarted by Carl Icahn, who gained the support of the board to throw Antioco out and move the company back to its core bricks and mortar business model. It may still have been too late to stop Netflix, but any chance of transforming Blockbuster's business model was blocked by Icahn and the board and, of course, the rest is history.

Let's also remember Steve Jobs' initial tenure at Apple. Jobs was the archetypal business model innovator constantly looking to reinvent the way value is created, delivered, and captured. There was a constant conflict at Apple between supporting the existing product line and reinventing it, with Jobs as the main cheerleader nudging to reinvent it. During Jobs' initial stay at Apple he brought in John Sculley, who was the president of PepsiCo, to become the Apple CEO in 1983. The dance between the two of them lasted 10 years, with Jobs always pushing for breakthrough product and service lines and Sculley trying to lean against him to stabilize the Apple business model. Jobs would not be stabilized and went to war against Sculley. In their now well-publicized battle, Jobs tried to get Sculley fired but in the end the board supported Sculley and Jobs was the one who ended up leaving first. Of course, Jobs got it right the second time around and went on to create the most amazing business model innovation factory ever seen, but in his first attempt he didn't have the full support of the board and the business model innovator was forced out. Business model innovation requires support from the top.

Staffing a Business Model Innovation Factory

A business model innovation factory should be staffed with innovation junkies. Innovators and designers, who are comfortable hanging out on the edge, are wired to always find a better way and to thrive on experimentation and change. A mix of innovators from inside and outside of the company is ideal. If a business model innovation factory is staffed exclusively with innovators from outside of the organization it will have great difficultly with the connected part of connected adjacency. If everyone comes from the outside it will be very difficult without existing relationships with executives inside of the core business model to gain access to capabilities necessary for many business model experiments. Even with support from the CEO and the board it helps to have existing relationships within the organization to leverage both knowledge and capabilities resident in the core business. Remember most new business models don't require the invention of new capabilities, just the freedom to combine and recombine them with capabilities from outside of the organization in novel ways to create, deliver, and capture value. A business model innovation factory is a connected adjacency with access to capabilities from the existing business model with the flexibility to redeploy them in business model experiments that test new configurations.

The opposite is also true. You don't want a business model innovation factory staffed only with people from within the organization. It is important to add new skills, perspectives, and approaches to the mix. Outside innovation and design talent can be sourced to support a business model innovation factory either by hiring directly into the organization or collaborating with a design, consulting, or innovation services firm. There are many firms with the skills and experience to help. Most are better at supporting specific projects than providing access to their innovation and design talent on an ongoing basis, but I expect business models of service firms will also evolve to support changing corporate business model innovation needs.

The real trick is how to identify and attract innovators from in and out of the organization to your business model innovation factory. Can you recognize an innovator when you meet one? The old adage, you can tell a pioneer because they are the ones with the arrows in their backs, may be true but doesn't help to identify innovators. I used to think we could convert everyone to be an innovator and create a culture in which everyone can. I have changed my view after many years as a road warrior consultant and innovation junkie. Proselytizing doesn't work. People are either wired as innovators or they aren't. The trick isn't to create more innovators, it is to identify them, connect them together in purposeful ways, and give them the freedom, tools, and resources to innovate. A leader's job is to create an environment where innovators can thrive.

Not everyone can or needs to be an innovator. I hear many executives express a desire to create a culture where all of their employees can innovate. I think that is the wrong objective. It is not important or even possible to have everyone in an organization innovate. In fact, most of the people in an organization should not be focused on innovation, they should be focused on delivering results within the current business model. These are the motivated and valued individuals committed to making quarterly numbers and annual business objectives. There is nothing wrong with that and these individuals must be highly valued in any organization. They get stuff done. They should not be made to feel like second-class citizens just because they are not innovators. Without them there would be no resources available to invest in innovation. Don't get me wrong, all individuals in any organization should be encouraged to be creative in doing their work as efficiently as they can and encouraged to contribute new ideas to improve the organization, but you don't want everyone in the company distracted by early stage ideas to transform or significantly change the business model.

Some part, not all, of your organization and allocated resources should be focused on business model innovation. Not just R&D for new products and services but R&D to develop new business models. Survival is dependent on constantly looking for ways to deliver more value to customers. Every organization should have a discreet business model innovation effort sponsored and resourced by senior leadership. Without this commitment, all business model innovation efforts will migrate toward incremental improvements to the current business model. Those are important, but should not crowd out potential game-changing growth opportunities, even ones that might disrupt the current business model.

If the game is to identify and connect innovators, how do you identify them and ensure that they have the resources and freedom to innovate? I like hanging around innovators and have been honing my targeting and selection process over many years. Here are 10 behavioral characteristics I use to recognize an innovator.

1. Innovators always think there is a better way.
2. Innovators know that without passion there can be no innovation.
3. Innovators embrace change to a fault.
4. Innovators have a strong point of view but know that they are missing something.
5. Innovators know that innovation is a team sport.
6. Innovators embrace constraints as opportunities.

7. Innovators celebrate their vulnerability.
8. Innovators openly share their ideas and passions, expecting to be challenged.
9. Innovators know that the best ideas are in the gray areas between silos.
10. Innovators know that a good story can change the world.

Identifying innovators and connecting them together in purposeful ways is the secret sauce for business model innovation. Change begins with the ability to recognize an innovator when you meet one.

Skills and Experience to Staff a Business Model Innovation Factory

A business model innovation factory is a platform, not a project. It enables an ongoing stream of new business model ideas and experiments. It enables R&D for new business models. At steady state it will have the resources and staff to lead and support a portfolio of business model innovation experiments going on at the same time. There will be a mix of projects going on in the business model innovation factory at any point in time, including some in the early concept development phase as well as business model experiments that are in later stage real-world testing. The main skills and experiences for key staff assigned to a business model innovation factory should include idea generators, ethnographers, and business model designers.

Idea Generators

Coming up with new business model ideas is the easy part. The hard part is getting ideas from the whiteboard onto a real-world test bed. Nonetheless, most of the innovation efforts I have observed within corporations think that coming up with good ideas is the hard part. It isn't. The first initiative of newly formed corporate innovation groups is almost always a modern-day version of a suggestion box. I have watched many companies anxious to put in place a platform welcoming innovation ideas from across the company. It is a good thing to encourage everyone in the organization to contribute ideas. In order to keep employees interested in continuing to contribute ideas and for them to contribute their really good ideas they will have to see that something is going to happen with their ideas and believe it is in their best interest to contribute them.

Just implementing a crowd source ideation solution by putting in place a process enabling employees to contribute their ideas won't work unless management really wants the ideas and intends to do something with the good ones. Ideation platforms only work if combined with new management process and leadership behavior change. The ideas that come from and are supported by senior management can't be the only ideas that count. Nothing kills crowd source ideation faster than watching your ideas sink to the bottom of an e-suggestion box ignored by management.

It is also important to create a separate ideation process for new business model ideas from sourcing ideas to improve the current business model. A general ideation or brainstorming process looking for innovation ideas is destined to produce lots of ideas to strengthen the current business model but is highly unlikely to produce ideas for entirely new business models. If you want business model innovation ideas you have to frame the questions you ask appropriately to focus ideation on concepts that have the potential to completely change the way the organization creates, delivers, and captures value. Business model ideation can't be constrained by perspectives driven by the current business model. The best way to ensure new perspectives is to go beyond internally generated ideas to also source new business model innovation concepts by bringing in ideas from outside the organization.

New business model ideas are most likely to be found in unusual places and by unusual suspects. The best ideas and value-creating opportunities are in the gray areas between silos, disciplines, and sectors. It is essential to get out more. Stop going to all the usual trade shows where you will only hear the same ideas from the same industry participants year after year. Start hanging out at the edge, going to events that convene the unusual suspects from industries and sectors that you would not normally interact with. You might learn something new there. You might collide with someone who is in a completely different environment but trying something new that may just be the idea that will spark an entirely new business model approach. One of the most important activities of any business model innovation factory is to take the organization out to the edges to explore new sources of knowledge and experience that can trigger ideas that would not have come through interacting with just the usual suspects.

Ethnographers: Voice and Experience of the Customer

No matter how many different ways I have tried over the years to focus the discussion at innovation brainstorming sessions on creating new business model concepts, I find the conversation inevitably migrates back to incremental ideas. No matter how I framed the question, participants were looking at the challenge through the lens of their current business model. Business model innovators need a new lens. They need a way to change their perspective from thinking about value through the lens of the current business model to thinking about value through the lens of the customer.

Think about all the conference room tables you have sat around hoping to talk about breakthrough innovation ideas only to have the discussion slide back toward incremental change. The main reason this happens is because the frame of reference for everyone around the table is the business model they are currently working in. Our current business models are ingrained in all us and we are wired to think and behave in ways that are consistent with them. Our organization's performance metrics, incentives, and performance management practices are all designed to reinforce the constraints of the current business model. It isn't a surprise that innovation discussions always end up with ideas to strengthen the current business model and tend to rule out ideas that represent a new model with the potential to cannibalize or disrupt the way the model works today.

When presented with a new technology that could potentially open up new business model opportunities, the strong tendency is to figure out ways to use the technology as a sustaining innovation to improve the current business model's performance. All new ideas are viewed through the current business model lens with perspectives that are biased to shape new ideas in ways that fit with the current model. The most important step in any business model innovation process is to find a way to change the lens we look through to assess new opportunities. The best way to do that is to see opportunities through the lens of the customer. Business model innovators have the ability to leave behind their current business model perspectives and biases to start anew with fresh perspectives that come from seeing the world through the lens of the end-user.

A business model innovation factory brings the voice and experience of the customer into the center of the innovation process. It establishes a deep foundation of understanding about the customer experience using ethnographic research and direct observational methods to uncover not just what the customer says they want or need but the actual behaviors surrounding the job an end-user is trying to do. Business model innovation is about designing a new way to create, deliver, and capture value around the end-user. Don't start with the way your organization creates, delivers, and captures value today. Start with the customer experience and the job-to-be-done and design new models around the end-user.

Any business model innovation factory must have the capability to build and sustain a strong foundation to bring the voice and experience of the customer to the center of all activities in the lab. It is not a discreet market research activity but an ongoing effort to understand and design around the end-user experience. The way to get out of the biases of the current business model is by walking in the shoes of the customer and identifying ways to enhance or change their experience unconstrained by the rules, processes, and financial requirements of the way the organization works today.

Business Model Designers

Business model innovation is a design process. It took me awhile to figure this out as a classically trained MBA who was taught that everything can be organized sequentially—first you do step A then step B then step C. I grew up in the corporate world where, however wrongheaded, we believed everything could be perfectly planned out and measured against financial hurdles and expectations in advance before starting any innovation project. Business model innovation doesn't work that way. Design doesn't work that way. Design is generative, experimental, and iterative. It is impossible to really know what step B and step C might be in advance. All good business model designers start with a compelling design challenge and a reasonable step A to start. Subsequent steps will emerge during the iterative design process as new observations and learning is brought into the design as it unfolds. Business model innovation should be based largely on design thinking, a way of thinking that's been core to the design process for many years, and more recently, has begun influencing everything from Fortune 500 companies, to top business schools, to social change.

There are many reasons a business model innovation factory should think and act like a designer, including the following.

New business models change the way customers experience things. Business model innovation begins with a deeper understanding of human behaviors, motivations, and experiences within a system. With a human-centered focus, it is possible to gain entirely new perspectives and ways to address customer needs and jobs-to-be-done. A human-centered focus generates powerful new insights. It also enables end-users, those at the center of any experience, to play a direct role in the business model design and development process itself.

Design process forces us to shift from the industrial-era approach of going from thinking to doing to an approach more relevant in the constantly changing twenty-first century, going from doing to think-ing. We learn by doing. Thinking informs doing and doing informs thinking. You can't start with the answer and set out to prove it's right. Design thinking suggests it is more important to experiment, to try things, learn what works, apply it, and measure its impact.

Design thinking enables us to more readily bring disparate ele-ments and ideas together. Business model design is about recombin-ing capabilities that don't normally go together. It enables us to borrow from different fields and disciplines and to recombine capa-bilities in new ways and across domains.

Design thinking challenges the meaning of existing models and systems. Design is one of the best ways we know to shift the way a problem is understood, generate new insights and options, and to create new value.

The following section is a sample job posting for a business model designer that would staff a business model innovation factory.

Wanted: Business Model Designers

The business model designer role is an opportunity to work at the intersection of human-centered design and business innovation. This role requires an ability to take the lead on design efforts to re-imagine, develop, and test new business model concepts.

As a Business Model Designer you will design for change by:

- Leading and contributing to ethnographic fieldwork to gener-ate powerful customer experience observations and insights.
- Leading and contributing to design teams through analysis and synthesis of ethnographic work to distill the most important insights leading to transformational business model concepts.
- Developing testable business model concepts and prototypes.
- Leading and contributing to real-world business model experiments.
- Creating and implementing frameworks to measure results and impact of business model experiments.

- Crafting and executing compelling multimedia stories that help stakeholders understand and connect with the work.
- Capturing and packaging learning from business model experiments to inform other efforts and ensure maximum leverage.

The ideal candidate:

- Is passionate about putting customer experience at the center of design efforts.
- Has a diverse background stemming from experience in domains including service design, industrial design, interaction design, communications design, environmental design, business model, and organizational design.
- Demonstrates mastery of the human-centered design process.
- Is interested in exploring new and novel business model concepts.
- Has an entrepreneurial mind-set and is comfortable working with ambiguous problems in a dynamic environment.
- Is able to work collaboratively and has a high threshold for ambiguity.

This role of business model designer requires a unique blend of research chops and real-world experience at the intersection of human-centered design and business innovation. You will work as a member of a business model design team to conceive of, develop, and test transformative approaches to creating, delivering, and capturing customer value.

Resourcing a Business Model Innovation Factory

In addition to the right skills and experience to staff a business model innovation factory, it is important to discuss how it should be funded and how business model projects are selected to work on. If the sole objective of a corporate innovation department is to improve the company's current business model, it makes sense to finance innovation activities with funds allocated to projects approved by line management from the core business. In that scenario the innovation function can be held accountable for its ability to produce either revenue creating or operating cost reduction opportunities that are aligned with the objectives of leaders responsible for improving the performance of the current business model. Line executives are most comfortable with this approach to managing an innovation agenda because it becomes straightforward analysis to measure the return on investment from any innovation project. Leaders from the sponsoring business unit or function apply the same financial metrics and benchmarks used to assess any alternative investment project trying to achieve the desired balance between projects with short and longer-term payoffs.

Of course, projects with shorter-term payoffs will always starve out those with longer-term returns, regardless of the potential. Innovation projects that require sign-off or are dependent on resources provided by leaders with day-to-day responsibility for running the current business model are held to the same financial standards and requirements as any other potential investment. It should then be no surprise to anyone that only those projects that look attractive to business unit and functional leaders based on short-term return and impact to the current business model are chosen and funded. It is also no surprise that any innovation project that has the potential to distract or disrupt the current business model is never chosen. Only those projects that will produce outcomes that make sense to the stakeholders in the existing business model get done. This approach may be necessary and appropriate to sustain and strengthen a company's current business model, but will not result in business model innovation.

If the strategic objective is business model innovation, resources must be allocated directly to support R&D for new business models. If resources are allocated to a broad innovation agenda with the intention to fund both projects to support the current business model and to develop new business models with the decision of which projects to support made by line management, the business model innovation projects will never get funded. Resources to finance business model experiments can't be dependent on approvals from line management that have no interest in creating new business models, especially those that might disrupt their current empires and operations. Resources for a business model innovation factory must be allocated outside of the budgeting process to support the current business model. The same is true for decision making on a business model innovation project portfolio. A committee made up of line executives will only result in steering projects toward activities to support the current business model and away from projects that might disrupt it. A business model innovation factory must be sponsored and supported by the CEO and the board of directors.

Overcoming the Politics of Business Model Innovation

If Blockbuster had a business model innovation factory before they were netflixed, could they have avoided the fate of being disrupted? Blockbuster had all the information and capabilities needed to avoid being disrupted. What got in their way were constraints of their current business model and the inability to overcome the internal politics and vested interests to protect the way their current business model worked. Blockbuster should have been experimenting with new ways to deliver movies to people's homes that didn't depend on their bricks and mortar locations. In order to do it they would have needed a business model innovation factory with the resources and autonomy to demonstrate how a new business model would work. They would have also needed senior leadership to support the activity even when line management raised concerns about potential cannibalization to try to stop the experiment. Business model innovation fails because of the politics of protecting the current business model. If Blockbuster had done the design, prototyping, and testing of a mail-order movie business model before Netflix arrived on the scene they would have been in a better position to run a separate mail-order business unit, spin off a new business retaining a stake, replace the bricks and mortar model, or at the very least they would have had a much better understanding of the competitive threat.

The threat of cannibalization is an unacceptable reason for not doing development work on potentially disruptive business models. Your business model is going to be disrupted whether your organization gets ahead of it or not. If you don't explore new business models a competitor will. It is likely to be an unexpected competitor that doesn't play by existing industry and business model rules. It is also likely to be a competitor without the same political and cost structure baggage that causes your organization to lean against or block any new business model idea that is a threat to your existing one. In the twenty-first century R&D for new business models isn't a nice thing to do, it's a must-do to avoid being disrupted. Disrupting yourself is so much better than being disrupted.

If Sony had a business model innovation factory would the Apple iPod and iTunes business model have been so successful at disrupting them and the entire music industry? The same pattern can be observed over and over again as companies are disrupted because they don't have the capability to do R&D for new business models. Existing business models and business unit structures get in the way. In Sony's case it had all the information and capabilities needed to disrupt itself, as well as the entire music industry, building on its leadership positions in consumer electronics and music. It was Sony's business unit operating structure, internal politics, and an inability to experiment with new business models that created the opportunity for Steve Jobs and Apple to recreate the music business instead.

Sony had very strong global market positions and business units in both the consumer electronics and the music business. They pioneered portable music devices long before the iPod was even on the drawing board by introducing the Walkman, for heaven's sake.

Everyone I know had one! Sony's music division was one of the largest record labels in the industry, with many of the most popular recording artists under contract. Given their capabilities you would think Sony was in a perfect position to do what Jobs and Apple ultimately did. But like most large companies with multiple business units, they had no platform for reassembling the parts from across their business units. The consumer electronics division had a well-oiled business model and so did the music division. Both divisions were operating their respective business models as aggressively as they could, both pursuing new product and capability opportunities to strengthen them. Each saw the market through their respective business model lenses.

Sony had no business model innovation factory with the autonomy to design and test novel ways to create, deliver, and capture value in the music industry. If they had, and started by thinking about value through the lens of the music consumer instead of through the lens of two separate business units, they would have seen opportunities to shape new business models. If they had a business model innovation factory with access to core capabilities across the two business units and the skills and resources to prototype and test new business model configurations, it stands to reason they might have explored a model that integrated a cool portable device with the consumer's favorite music easily accessible on it.

When Apple developed their iPod/iTunes integrated business model they didn't have a music division owning the rights to the popular music the way Sony did. Apple had to convince record labels to work with them. Sony wouldn't have had to convince anyone outside the company to at least demonstrate the new model. All they had to do was reach into their own two business units and reassemble the parts in a different way. Easier said than done for most companies. A business model innovation factory may have prevented Sony from being embarrassed and disrupted by Apple. It would have taken strong leadership at the top with the commitment to overcome internecine politics intent on blocking business model innovation.

9 Experimenting with Business Models in the Real World

Consumer product companies have long employed test markets to trial new products and new marketing campaigns in the real world before risking national or global rollout. Consumer product marketers have long looked for representative conditions and demographics as test markets to provide a good understanding of the way a product will be received by the market by simulating as closely as possible actual commercialization conditions. They don't rely solely on traditional market research studies including conjoint analyses to identify product feature trade-offs, customer surveys and focus groups, price sensitivity studies, and focus groups. Consumer product marketers want to know how the product will do in real market conditions. Marketing mix can only be optimized based on observing real market performance, not on the results of quantitative and qualitative market research reports and what consumers say they will do behind the two-way glass of a focus group facility. Real market experience is required. Why not employ the same approach to explore and test new business models?

It's easy to come up with new business model ideas on paper. It's easy to do pro-forma analyses of how a new business model might work. It's easy to write fancy reports embellishing the potential of a hypothetical new business model. None of these theoretical exercises matters without testing new business model concepts in the real world. Until a business model idea sees the light of day in the real world it is impossible to know if it will work. Business model concepts always end up working differently in the real world than first imagined on the whiteboard, presentation deck, or business plan.

Just talk to any successful serial entrepreneur about their experience of starting a new business. If you observe serial entrepreneurs launching new businesses they almost never get the business model right on the first try. It takes several iterations to find a business model that works on the ground and has the potential to scale. Their initial concept is almost never the one that ultimately succeeds. Serial entrepreneurs will tell you it's a waste of time writing a fancy business plan that details all of the components of a proposed new business model. What is contained within the initial plan will have little to no bearing on what business model will ultimately gain traction and work under real market conditions. It would be far better to sketch out the business model concept on the back of a napkin and move as quickly as possible into the market to see if the business model holds up in the real world.

The goal is to move as quickly as possible from concept to prototype to test and then iterate until landing on a business model configuration that works and is ready to scale. Along the way there will be many failures. The trick, of course, is to fail fast and to capture learning that can be applied to future business model experiments. Corporate business model innovators can learn a lot by observing successful serial entrepreneurs.

Mickey Drexler, chairman and CEO of J. Crew Group, and formerly the CEO of Gap Inc., serves on the board of Apple and gave Steve Jobs some excellent advice that is relevant for any business model innovator. Jobs was getting frustrated with Apple's inability to control the entire customer experience with its products being sold through traditional consumer electronic retail channels. Jobs didn't think Apple products were getting the shelf placement, sales support, and customer service they deserved and wanted to apply Apple's design magic to what he rightly believed was a critical part of the customer experience, buying the product. As Jobs began thinking about how to take control of the customer purchase experience by opening up direct Apple stores, Mickey Drexler told him to build a prototype of the Apple Store near the Apple campus and to hang out there until he was comfortable with it. Drexler gave Jobs the perfect advice and that is exactly what Apple did. It created a real-world lab or design studio to explore how the new business model would work.

While the new business model was being designed and tested the rest of the organization was still driving the existing business model and retail channels. It was essential to do both while determining if the new business model made sense, could work in the real world, and could scale. Apple made many changes to the store configuration during the design phase. Walter Isaacson, in his biography of Steve Jobs, describes how all of the initial planning for the model Apple Store called for a floor layout designed around product groupings. The first tendency of all product companies is to imagine the customer experience through the lens of their current business models. So of course the initial Apple Store layout was organized around product groupings. But Steve Jobs realized late in the store design process that the customer experience wasn't about product groupings—it was about what consumers were doing and could do with Apple products. Despite the fact that the store design was all but complete and the Apple team was hurdling toward the planned launch date for the first Apple Store, Jobs and Ron Johnson, who was in charge of the project, both realized the Apple Store design would have to be completely redone.

The Apple Store story points out several important lessons for business model innovators. Even though the core Apple business model at the time was organized around retail partners, Jobs did not allow executives in the core business model, who would be completely disrupted by the creation of a direct sales channel through Apple Stores, to block the experiment with and ultimate move to an entirely new business model. Imagine the push back from line executives accountable to manage and strengthen Apple's relationships with their retail partners. All of their goals, incentives, and operating norms were aligned to the existing retail distribution business model. Even the idea of an Apple Store must have been incredibly threatening to the way work got done every day at Apple. Business model innovation is about experimenting with new models, even those that might disrupt the current one, while continuing to operate within the existing business model.

The Apple Store story also demonstrates the importance of real-world prototyping and experimentation. It was by creating a real-world prototype and launching the initial stores that Apple was able to iterate toward the winning customer experience that ultimately became the hallmark of Apple's new business model. The prototype store was a connected adjacency that had the autonomy to design and test an entire new approach to deliver the Apple customer experience and yet it had enough of a connection to the core business to leverage capabilities necessary to run the experiment. The key is the ability to freely reassemble and play with parts in novel ways. The Apple Store really didn't invent anything new other than an entirely new way to deliver value through a compelling customer experience. The capabilities to make it happen already existed—it took leadership, a compelling vision, a consumer-centric design approach, willingness to experiment with new configurations, and a real-world platform to try out new business model designs.

I first became interested in the idea of real-world business model experimentation at the end of a consulting project I led for the CEO of one of my pharmaceutical company clients. The CEO had asked us to develop a series of recommendations on how they could improve their company's position within the diabetes market. The company had several diabetes products in the market at the time and several others in their development pipeline. The CEO had identified the diabetes market as a strategic growth opportunity for the company and tasked our consulting team with developing what he called "transformational solutions." "Think outside-of-the-box" he told us, which was what every client said at the beginning of every project so we were skeptical that he really wanted true breakthrough ideas. Most didn't really mean it. What they really wanted were ideas that fit within their current business models, including new product opportunities and ways to strengthen their existing capability set.

In this case we delivered a range of solutions including both ideas that were traditional and in alignment with the current pharmaceutical industry business model, and ideas that represented transformational change and opportunities for entirely new business models. I remember one idea we detailed in our fancy consulting deck, which was to move from a product-focused business model to one that was focused on delivering patient outcomes: an outcomes-based business model that delivered a portfolio of products and services to diabetics, enabling them to better control and manage their own disease. Instead of selling them products, the idea was to help them better manage their disease through a personalized approach that only provided those products and services necessary for the specific individual. The outcomes-based business model idea proposed was to explore a go-to-market approach where instead of getting paid by selling products, revenue would be generated by producing favorable patient outcomes or when patients could better control and manage their diabetes.

In the currently prevailing pharmaceutical business model the company gets paid for their products regardless of whether they work or not or whether the patient is better able to manage their disease or not. In an outcomes-based business model the company would deploy the necessary products and services required to achieve patient success. The idea we proposed was a business model that shifted from selling drugs to selling patient outcomes. Well, no surprise to anyone on our consulting team or within the company we were working for, the CEO thanked us for all of the ideas and proceeded to select and implement those that fit within their current business model. "We are a product company," he proclaimed, "and we will remain a product company."

Well, I am not one to leave things alone and couldn't resist pushing the idea. I wondered out loud if he would be willing to try the idea, to experiment with the new outcomes-based business model at a small scale to see if it was viable. I even blurted out, "Give me Rhode Island." I was living in Rhode Island at the time and said, "You don't care about Rhode Island, it's too small to matter to your business but big enough to test a new business model in the real world. An experiment won't affect your quarterly earnings or share price. Give me Rhode Island to design, prototype, and test an outcomes-based business model and I will demonstrate to you how the model can work and how you can make money at it. If it works you will be in a position to decide if it makes sense to scale or not." The CEO listened but in the end said, "no thanks" and stuck with the tried and true pharmaceutical industry business model. I have never forgotten the discussion or the idea of creating real-world platforms for business model experimentation.

Give Me Rhode Island

The key to experimenting with new business model concepts is creating the conditions in the real world to enable a realistic simulation of how the business model works. It isn't good enough to conduct market research to ask potential customers if they would alter their purchasing behavior from a hypothetical business model. A business model innovation factory enables a real-world demonstration in actual market conditions to determine the viability and attractiveness of a new business model concept. The imperative is to quickly take business model concepts off of the whiteboard and put them into the real world to see if they work. Little did I know when I suggested to my client CEO, "Give me Rhode Island" that years later I would come back to the idea.

After retiring from Accenture I found myself catching my breath from many years traveling around the world as a road warrior consultant. I lived in Rhode Island but I hadn't spent much time over the years paying attention to the local community as I was traveling to clients and to Accenture offices around the world most weeks. Now I was back hanging out in Rhode Island trying to figure out what I was going to do next, and it turns out that my family really wasn't in the market for a strategy consultant at home to advise on household operations. I had to find something else to do and didn't want to relocate or to travel as much as I had been doing. I started to look, really look, at my local community for the first time. I had spent my entire career in the private sector, and as an innovation junkie had always thought about and practiced innovation through the lens of a corporation. For the first time in my career I began to think about innovation through the lens of a community. Wow. What a perspective change.

I raised my hand to Donald Carcieri, the then-newly elected governor of Rhode Island, and to Michael McMahon, executive director of the state's economic development agency, and the next thing I knew I went to work for the agency. I started with responsibility for the agency's business development activity, and when Michael McMahon left to return to Wall Street with a private equity firm, Governor Carcieri asked me to join his cabinet, lead the agency, and become his Executive Counselor for Economic and Community Development. I had become an accidental bureaucrat after many years in the private sector successfully avoiding the public sector!

Rhode Island is an amazing place if you are an innovation junkie like me. It is the smallest state in the country with about a million people jammed into a little over a thousand square miles. Everyone knows everyone. There can't be more than two degrees of separation between any two Rhode Islanders. I literally could see the entire movie that is Rhode Island from my office window. I could observe the way all the moving parts across the public and private sector maneuvered around the chessboard. I could see the way companies did or did not interact with government, colleges, and universities. The state looked and felt like a potential innovation platform to me. Hypothetically, I reasoned, it should be easier in Rhode Island to innovate, to connect the dots across silos in our small state to explore and test new business models and social systems.

I launched an economic development strategy I called innovation @ scale to turn the entire state into an innovation hotspot, a place that innovators could more easily take new business model concepts off the whiteboard and get them in to the real world to see if they worked and could operate successfully at scale. My argument was that by activating the state as a real-world test bed we would be turning our state's small size from a disadvantage to a strategic advantage. Citizens would benefit from both access to new solutions and a stronger economy as local companies leveraged the test bed to get stronger nationally and globally and as innovative companies from outside the state were attracted to and invested in our unique real-world innovation lab. As small countries in Northern Europe and in the Far East have learned, if you are small you have no choice but to be good.

Much of the thinking in this book about the imperative to do R&D for new business models and the real-world conditions necessary to enable it come from my economic development work in Rhode Island, and now that I am back in the private sector, where I belong, from the work we do around the world applying these principles at the Business Innovation Factory. I spent six years as an accidental bureaucrat promoting innovation @ scale across Rhode Island. We started an important public conversation about the economic future of Rhode Island that continues today, and I am proud of the progress we made during incredibly difficult economic conditions. I have come to believe that this economic development approach isn't just appropriate for Rhode Island but is applicable to any community that wants to recreate its economic future by becoming an innovation hotspot.

Along the way I learned a lot about what it really means to create the conditions for business model and social system experimentation. It is clear that the conditions start by finding and collaborating with leaders who want to innovate and not just protect the status quo. The conditions for business model experimentation also include working with those institutions that have the capacity and motivation for trying new things, not just tweaks to the way things work today but trying true transformational approaches. It is also important that the institutions you choose to collaborate with on business model experiments have the collaboration muscle to work effectively across silos, sectors, and disciplines. The rhetoric is easy but getting below the buzzwords to conduct successful business model innovation experiments only works with collaborators that have demonstrated capacity for experimentation.

Another lesson I learned during the time I spent as an accidental bureaucrat is that proselytizing doesn't work. You can't convince people and institutions that don't want to change to innovate. My experience has taught me that it is far better to find people and institutions that want to innovate and are receptive to experimentation and change and then to enable them with the tools and platforms to accomplish it. I came to understand that the conditions for real-world business model experimentation can be found and created anywhere, not just in Rhode Island. Every community has the potential to become an innovation hotspot and every company needs to access the conditions to experiment with new business models in the real world. Every company with a business model innovation factory needs access to communities where they can experiment with novel business models in the real world. Smart communities will position themselves as innovation platforms for these companies. It is a match made in heaven and a formula for both more competitive, growing, and job-producing companies and for more prosperous communities relevant to a twenty-first century global economy.

A Better Place

One of the best examples of both business model innovation and the importance of a real-world test bed to develop it is the company Better Place founded by Shai Agassi. In 2005 Agassi attended the World Economic Forum (WEF) in Davos, Switzerland. He was inspired by a framing question asked by WEF's founder Klaus Schwab at the beginning of the conference, "How do you make the world a better place by 2020?" Agassi took Schwab's question seriously and decided he would make the world a better place by reducing the world's dependence on oil by creating market-based infrastructure to support a transition to all electric cars. I love that he called the company Better Place.

Agassi knew that the only way to accomplish his goal was through business model innovation and industry system change. The existing business models that comprise the current gas-powered automobile-based transportation systems around the world would all have to be transformed to make an electric car system work. Transformational business model change would be necessary for all industry players, including car manufacturers, car battery manufacturing and supply, auto maintenance and repair, and the fuel retailing business. Each component of our current car transportation system has its own well-developed and entrenched business model with companies who all compete on a well-defined set of industry practices. It isn't technology that is getting in the way of transitioning to an all-electric car transportation system and reducing our global dependency on oil, it is the entrenched business models of the current auto industry and the way they create, deliver, and capture value that is in the way.

Existing companies in the auto industry are focused on strengthening their current business models and competitive positions within their respective industry segments. Each segment (cars, batteries, gas, service, finance) has a comfortable place within the current industry structure and it's in all of the competitor's best interests to maintain the industry status quo. To each current auto industry competitor innovation primarily means developing new products and services (a new car, auto part, or service) to create top-line revenue growth in order to increase their market share.

An electric car system is viewed as a disruption to all of the current industry competitors and the tendency is to do everything they can to resist and block it. An electric car industry system requires business model innovation and system change. It requires the ability to reassemble the parts in novel ways. It requires a business model innovation factory and a real-world test bed. It is easy to sketch out how it might work on the whiteboard but harder to test in the real world given how entrenched the current set of business models and competitors are within the current industry configuration. The imperative is to do R&D for a new electric car industry business model. On the business model innovation critical path is finding or creating the conditions in the real world to test the new business model concept.

Shai Agassi and Better Place set out to do exactly that, to take their idea from concept to a real-world test bed to prove that it could work and scale. Better Place found its real world test bed in both Israel and Denmark. In each of these locations Better Place found small compact countries with enlightened leaders who want to be recognized as innovators and who are willing to help create the conditions on the ground to experiment with an electric car system. In both Israel and Denmark, policies were enacted to help accelerate the transition by creating a tax differential between electric and traditional gas-fueled cars. In Israel, the first pilot location, Better Place announced an agreement with Renault-Nissan to provide the electric cars with swappable batteries while Better Place would develop an electric recharge grid and network of battery switch stations around the country.

The idea is to make swapping out batteries as easy as stopping at a gas station is today. People will be able to drive throughout the country and know they just have to pull into a battery swapping station to refuel. The range of the initial electric cars is from 100 to 120 miles with a single charge, and by locating battery switching stations throughout the country consumers will be able to travel freely, limited only by the distance from the nearest switching station the same way it works today with gas stations. The batteries will be swapped out robotically at a switching station in about two minutes, or less time than it takes to fill up a car with gas today. The driver never has to get out of the car. It will be like going through the drive-through at a fast-food restaurant or a carwash at the gas station.

The way Better Place intends to capture value with an innovative financial model concept is also transformational and must be tested in the real world. The Better Place business model calls for consumers to buy an electric car without a battery, the same way they would currently buy a car that comes without the gas necessary to fuel it. Consumers would then enter into a use contract for a swappable battery and access to recharging infrastructure with Better Place. The contract with Better Place will be based on the miles a consumer is planning to drive over the course of a year. There will be different usage level contracts available, ranging from light to heavy usage requirements. It would be similar to contracting with a cell phone company based on how much a consumer plans to use the phone. Rather than paying to fill the tank the way consumers do today in this business model, consumers would make monthly payments to cover all electric costs including the battery, daily charging, and swapping the battery at switching stations as needed. The Better Place economic model at scale provides consumers with both an electric car and access to the refueling infrastructure for less money than it costs today to purchase and maintain a gas-fueled car.

Agassi and the Better Place team envision a time when all of the electricity necessary to fuel the network in every country comes completely from renewable energy sources like solar and wind. In the interim they are partnering with Intel and Microsoft to create a smart software platform to enable the management of recharging all of the batteries so that it doesn't overload the local electric grid.

While it remains to be seen how the Better Place business model will work and scale across the world there is a lot of market interest and support for the concept. In 2010 Better Place raised $350 million, the largest venture capital raise of the year, and in 2011 they added another $200 million, bringing their total capital raise to $750 million to-date. Their first commercial nationwide electric car networks are planned to launch in 2012 in Israel and Denmark, with many interested countries and communities under development to follow.

The question for company executives in the auto industry or leaders with companies in any industry for that matter is, are you going to sit back and wait for companies like Better Place to disrupt you and the industry you compete in, or are you going to create a business model innovation factory to explore and test new business models on an ongoing basis? Are you a share taker or a market maker?

The most interesting business model innovation opportunities and the ones with the best value creation potential are usually networked business models that require the connection of capabilities across current industry sector boundaries. Just like the Better Place example, it requires the capacity to connect capabilities across silos and outside of the current organization boundaries to come up with new ways to create, deliver, and capture value. I have observed this pattern repeatedly over the years across companies and industries. Transformational opportunities almost always require reaching across traditional industry boundaries to explore novel ways to create value. Far too many transformational ideas never make it off the whiteboard because networked business model innovation concepts are outside of a company's comfort zone and business model wheelhouse. Even though the best potential collaborators are often not in the same industry sector and hence not direct competitors, most companies just don't have the collaboration muscle to pull it off. The internal hurdles and required approvals to try anything new are way too high to mobilize networked business model experiments. Legal, financial, and operating procedure constrains make it impossible to try new stuff. These constraints must be relaxed so a business model innovation factory can more easily network capabilities from both within and outside of a company to explore new business model configurations.

Most transformational ideas never make it off of the whiteboard. They are often testable propositions that could be explored given the right conditions to experiment with networked business model concepts in the real world. An example from my work in the pharmaceutical industry is the opportunity for an RFID (Radio

Frequency Identification) enabled pharmaceutical supply chain to ensure the pedigree and security of pharmaceutical products from raw material to your medicine cabinet. Everyone agrees that it makes sense to be able to track and trace pharmaceutical products throughout the supply chain to protect consumers against product tampering and counterfeiting, as well as ensure patient safety when products need to be located and recalled by either the company or a regulatory agency.

In order for an RFID enabled system to work, all of the players in the pharmaceutical value chain (pharmaceutical company, drug wholesaler, drug store) would need to coordinate activities and agree to align with industry standards. It isn't technology that is getting in the way of a transformed pharmaceutical supply chain because RFID technology has matured to the point where it can be deployed reliably and its price point has come down to where a high-value supply chain like pharmaceuticals could adopt it economically. What is getting in the way is the lack of aligned interests among different industry sector players, each with their own entrenched business model and vested interests. There is no agreement among industry players on how the value of transitioning to an RFID system is created and for whom, on how value would be delivered in a new system configuration, and how the value would be captured and paid for. It is a real rugby scrum and while an RFID enabled solution has been discussed for years, little real progress has been made to deploy it.

Each player in the current system points at everyone else in the system and leans against any real change. This example is typical in describing how existing business models and industry systems protect themselves and lean against any potentially disruptive technology or transformational change. Companies that want to lead transformation change are going to have to follow the Better Place example and create the real-world conditions to explore how the system might work and to evaluate alternative business model approaches, including how best to handle the costs of the required infrastructure to support the system and who will pay for it. An

RFID enabled pharmaceutical supply chain is a very testable proposition that has been debated and leaned against by current industry players for a long time. Only real-world experimentation of the new model will determine the ultimate value of deploying RFID technology for the pharmaceutical supply chain.

An important question is, can an existing pharmaceutical company, drug wholesaler, or chain drugstore lead the way to a transformed system, will a regulatory agency impose it upon the industry, or will a disruptive company or intermediary come along to do the business model experiment, creating an entire new business opportunity for itself the way Better Place is doing for electric vehicles? Could an existing car company have done what Better Place is doing to disrupt the existing industry model? I think it could but only if it embraced business model innovation and established the capacity to do ongoing R&D for new business models. Business models just don't last as long as they used to and all company leaders are going to have to get comfortable with business model experimentation or risk being disrupted by companies like Better Place.

Putting the Customer in the Business Model Driver Seat

Another important aspect of real-world business model experimentation is, whenever possible, to put the customer in the business model driver seat. Instead of designing a new business model and hoping that consumers will engage and embrace it, what if we actually enabled the consumers themselves to participate directly in the process? What if instead of just designing a new business model based on a deep understanding of the end-user experience we actually gave the design keys directly to the consumer and supported them in the design, prototyping, and testing of new business models? Perhaps if we enabled customers to design business models that best help them with the jobs they are attempting to do they would be more likely to support them, buy from them, and tell all of their friends to do the same. The trend toward self-organization and participative design is worth paying attention to and it's important that a business model innovation factory develop the tools to take advantage of the potential power to be unleashed by directly engaging the end-user, not only in the ideation and research phase of creating a new business model, but also in the design and testing of new business model concepts developed by and for the end-user themselves.

IV

Business Models Aren't Just for Business

10 Nonprofits Have Business Models Too

During my six years as an accidental bureaucrat, after spending 25 years in the private sector, my friends often wondered how I could do it. They routinely asked versions of the question, "Doesn't government move too slowly for you?" My standard reply was that, yes, the public sector moves slowly—but then, big companies don't move so quickly either. And come to think of it, I teased my friends in higher education, I'm sure that colleges and universities move more slowly than either business or government! The point is, all institutions move slowly.

What surprised me wasn't how slowly the different institutions moved, but the different language, behavior, secret handshakes, and views of each other I found across sectors. Xenophobia runs rampant within public, private, nonprofit, and for-profit silos. Each silo has created its own world completely foreign to inhabitants from other sectors. Visiting emissaries are always viewed with skepticism. We have all heard and maybe even uttered the following sentiments: "I'm from the government and I'm here to help to you"; "I'm from the social sector because someone has to save the world from itself"; "I'm from the private sector because someone has to be accountable for real results." It's enough to drive anyone trying to work across the sectors to solve complex social challenges crazy.

Each sector thinks they are the only one that really matters. Each sector views all the others with extreme skepticism, readily pointing fingers, blaming each other for being the obstacle to making real progress. If only the public and social sectors would get their act together. It's the fault of the greedy for-profit private sector. Everyone blames everyone else and the distrust escalates, making collaboration extremely difficult if not impossible. For all the times we hear the phrase "public private partnerships," you would think that collaboration across sectors was a normal and frequent occurrence. Everyone may talk about public private partnerships but in my experience few get below the buzzwords to actually connect capabilities across sector silos to change the way value is delivered. It's no surprise that none of the sectors share their toys well with the others. They just don't work and play nicely together.

One epiphany from my immersion into the public sector is how strenuously social sector organizations resist the notion they even have a business model. Nonprofits, government agencies, social enterprises, schools, and NGOs consistently proclaim that they aren't businesses, and therefore business rules don't apply. I heard this sentiment continuously from leaders in the public and social sector. Public sector leaders would constantly remind me, "Our objective isn't profit and therefore we aren't a business and have no intention of operating like one." Social sector leaders bristle at any mention of the word "business" associated with what their organizations do. I love the way government and social sector organizations react to people who come from the business world, like I did, and try to leverage business experience or infuse any notion of business practice into the social sector world. Talk about an antigenic response. While I blathered on during my time in the public sector most who were stuck listening would just nod their heads knowingly as if to say, I have seen many like you come and go thinking they could make us run more like a business, but you too will pass and I will wait you out. And they do!

Well, I'm sorry to break the news, but if an organization has a viable way to create, deliver, and capture value, it has a business model. It doesn't matter whether an organization is in the public or private sector. It doesn't matter if it's a nonprofit or a for-profit enterprise. All organizations have a business model. It may be that the business model is implicit and assumed rather than explicit and discussed openly. It's amazing how few organizations can clearly articulate their business model. Can yours? If you ask any 10 people in your organization how it creates, delivers, and captures value, will the answers even be close? If not, it's probably because, in the industrial era when business models seldom changed and everyone played the game by the same set of well-understood industry and sector rules, it wasn't as important to be explicit about business models. Business models were safely assumed and taken for granted.

That won't work in the twenty-first century, when all bets are off. Business models don't last as long as they used to. New players are rapidly emerging, enabled by disruptive technology, refusing to play by industrial-era rules. Business model innovators aren't constrained by existing business models. Business model innovation is becoming the new strategic imperative for all organization leaders regardless of what sector they operate in. This is as true for the public and social sector as it is for the private sector.

Nonprofit corporations may have a social mission and may not be providing a financial return to investors or owners, but they still capture value to finance activities with contributions, grants, and service revenue. Social enterprises may be mission-driven, focused on delivering social impact versus a financial return on investment, but they still need a sustainable model to scale. Government agencies are financed by taxes, fees, and service revenue, but are still accountable to deliver citizen value at scale.

The idea that business models are just for business is just wrong. Any organization that wants to be relevant, to deliver value at scale, and to sustain itself must clearly articulate and evolve its business model. And if an organization doesn't have a sustainable business model, it will not thrive in the twenty-first century. This applies to all organizations across both the public and private sector.

Nonprofits are feeling the lack of well-defined sustainable business models acutely during the current devastating economic downturn. The recession has been particularly harsh to the social sector. As philanthropic donations, government investment, and grant resources have become increasingly more difficult to secure and the demand for social services has dramatically increased, nonprofits everywhere have been squeezed. And because most have resisted the adoption of sound business practices they find themselves without a sustainable business model. It is incredibly sad to visit with so many important and well-intentioned organizations that have little to no capacity to develop a sustainable business model so they can scale their important work and weather the inevitable economic downturns.

I first realized how far apart the thinking and practice is across the public, social, and for-profit business sectors when a friend asked me to meet with his daughter, who had recently graduated from college and was passionate about her new work in a social enterprise, but (according to her father) had no clue about the private sector or business world. I agreed to do it and was floored when the first question she asked me was, how does work get funded in a private sector business? In her world all of the work done at the nonprofit social enterprise she worked for was funded by grants and donations. She seemed surprised when I explained to her that in the for-profit business sector, work was funded primarily by revenue from selling products and services valued by customers. While she certainly had experience as a consumer, she now saw the world entirely through the social enterprise lens, where all of the funding to support the social venture she was passionate about came from grants and donations. Revenue from delivering a product or service to a consumer was a foreign idea, given her lens. She had to really think about the two different concepts. This was a very well-educated person asking a serious question trying to understand the difference. We weren't talking about corporate structure for tax purposes or return on investment, we were talking about how value is created, delivered, and captured. We were talking about business models and how to sustain and scale them regardless of whether it is a for-profit or nonprofit business.

In our conversation I used the example of how most nonprofit hospitals and universities work. They clearly demonstrate that non-profits have business models too. In many communities, nonprofit hospitals and universities are now the largest businesses and employers. In the current economic downturn hospitals and univer-sities have proven to have the most resilient and sustainable busi-ness models within many communities. While they may be nonprofit corporate structures, they operate like any other business I have ever seen. Just check out the salaries of their CEOs and senior managers! Most of the revenue to support the operation of a non-profit hospital or university comes from services they provide to patients and students in the form of hospital and tuition bills. But if you examine their business models you will find they all have strengthened their business models by capturing additional finan-cial resources beyond service revenue through contributions and grants from philanthropic individuals, foundations, and govern-ment. These alternative revenue sources are critical to the overall success of their nonprofit business models, but they are additive on top of the core service revenue.

For most nonprofits in the social sector it is the other way around. Core revenue to support operations comes primarily from grants and donations. Trying to establish sustainable sources of ser-vice revenue is viewed as the alternative or gravy on top of the core. The current economic downturn is causing a world of hurt for many nonprofits that have watched funding sources shrivel up with no alternative to sustain the organization. Sadly, many well-intentioned and important nonprofits critical to the social fabric of the commu-nity have had to close their doors due to lack of a sustainable busi-ness model.

I have had varying versions of the same conversation with more nonprofit leaders than I can count. I always ask them to describe their business model. At first they resist the notion they have or need a business model. The conversation always starts with nonprofit leaders resisting the characterization of the important work they do as a business. Once I explain what a business model is and that every organization has one, including their nonprofit, they are usually quick to describe how they create and deliver value. Most are wonderfully passionate about the value they deliver and how important it is that they continue to fund the work. They are quick to describe how it is getting increasingly harder to find the funding. But when I ask how they plan to sustain their business model and if there are opportunities to develop ongoing service revenue to complement donation and grant investments, they aren't as quick to answer.

Most nonprofit leaders I have spoken with recognize they need to find alternative revenue sources but either resist the notion of service revenue or don't know how to identify and capture opportunities. They know how to run the current business model, supported by grants and donations, which has worked up to this point, but just like organization leaders in the private sector, they don't have the capacity to experiment with new business models while they are busy trying to get the current one to produce. That is going to have to change. We need the important work of many of these nonprofits to be sustainable and to scale within our communities. Tweaks to current nonprofit business models aren't enough. It will take business model innovation for many of them to survive and to thrive.

Any nonprofit totally dependent on grants to support its business model is at risk. Grants are a wonderful way to start a new program or to establish a new capability, but no matter how large the grants are or how many years they last they always run out. In my experience, the bigger the grant the more likely the nonprofit is to procrastinate establishing a sustainable business model. I have watched many nonprofits with the good fortune to land a substantial multi-year grant wait until it's too late to figure out how the organization can continue at its current size to deliver the valuable services it has been able to deliver with grant funding. Nonprofit leaders can see the cliff coming with grant expiration dates looming but seem unable to explore and test new business models as a path to sustainability. Instead they focus all of the organization's effort trying to convince the current funder to invest again or to find another source for a comparable grant. Most are unsuccessful in replacing the grant and have to go through a painful downsizing because new revenue sources haven't been identified. Nonprofit leaders are no different than leaders of all types of organizations. They fail to explore potential new business models while the current one is working well. The time to explore potential new business models is when the grant first comes in and there are resources available to support the effort.

Another problem with nonprofit business models that are dependent solely on grants to sustain themselves are the constraints that come with almost every grant. Most grant funding is to develop a specific program or to deliver a specific service within the community. The grant funds come with a straitjacket preventing the resources from being used for other purposes beyond those the grant is intended for. Most grants severely restrict the amount of funds that can be used to support overhead or platform investments that may be necessary to ensure sustainability beyond the grant period. So inevitably what happens is all of the grant resource is used to staff up and to establish the capabilities necessary to deliver on grant commitments defined in minute detail within the grant agreement. So the organization gets completely focused on delivering on the grant objectives and doesn't spend the necessary time establishing a platform that would enable the nonprofit to continue to deliver the intended service beyond the initial grant period. You would think it is in both the grantor and the grantees mutual interest to create a sustainable business model, but rarely are the resources necessary to do it built into the grant.

Nonprofits jump through amazing hoops to land the next grant. When a grant request for proposal (RFP) is dangled in front of social sector leaders, everyone stops what they are doing and the troops rally to try and win the grant. I have even seen real collaboration across the social sector when a significant grant opportunity calls for partners with different capabilities in order to qualify. It is amazing to see how well disparate partners can work together when potential grant funding is at stake. Really good collaborative solutions and new potential ways to solve social problems come out of these grant proposal processes. I have always thought if we want to enable more networked business models across organizations and sectors, funders should make collaboration among multiple partners a requirement for all funding.

I experimented with this approach while I worked in state government creating and securing the funding to enable a collaborative research grant program to try to get the eleven colleges and universities in the state of Rhode Island to actually work together. Eleven colleges and universities jammed into Rhode Island's small 1,000 square mile footprint and I found very little interaction and collaboration between them. What a huge strategic advantage it would be if all of them were networked together in a purposeful way. We created a collaborative grant program to fund and incent research initiatives within target innovation areas including life science, marine and environmental science, IT, and digital media and design. We told the research community we would only consider proposals that came from two or more colleges and universities collaborating in substantive ways on the work.

Imagine the indignation that we would try to constrain access to the funds requiring that they actually work together. At first the institutions thought we were kidding and that they could submit proposals with only a perfunctory mention of a researcher from another university. But we weren't kidding and stuck to the collaborative objective. It worked—the program is still going, connecting numerous researchers and research programs together that previously had no clue the others existed, even in the tiny state of Rhode Island. These new collaborations across the state and the funds invested locally to catalyze the activity have been leveraged to go after and receive significant additional federal funds. Collaboration muscle is an important community asset.

Grants are a good way to incent the development of collaboration muscle. But I noticed teams that had worked so well together and came up with compelling collaborative approaches and solutions during the proposal process disbanded immediately if the grant didn't come through. After the dejection of not getting a grant, I would try to tell the proposal team members that they had pulled together an amazing team and came up with very valuable collaborative solutions, but before I could get to the part about keeping the team together and exploring alternative funding sources and business models to move their idea forward despite being turned down for the grant, they had already disbanded and gone back to their respective organizations in search of the next grant opportunity.

Seems a shame to depend only on grant funding to bring together capabilities from across organizations. If collaborative ideas have the potential to deliver real value and solve real-world problems there should be alternative ways to attract resources or to finance the effort. The same is true for nonprofit business models relying exclusively on grant funding. Sustainability will be extremely difficult depending on only one source of revenue to support it. Of course when a nonprofit wins a grant, after a brief celebration and deep sigh of relief, all of the effort is typically focused on delivery on the grant objectives, with little to no effort focused on creating a sustainable business model. So the boom and bust cycle continuously repeats itself, constrained by access to grant money.

Government agencies have business models too. Government agencies work the same way nonprofit business models do—just substitute taxpayer dollars for grants. I get the same reaction from government leaders that I get from those in the social sector to the notion that government agencies have a business model with a healthy dose of "you too will pass." It's true. Government agencies have to create, deliver, and capture value just like any other business model. As citizens and taxpayers we are government's business model customers. The cynics among us might say government has the capture part down and could use a little work on the value creation and delivery part!

After experiencing the hard-wired inefficiencies baked into government agencies firsthand on a small scale in Rhode Island, I began to use an analogy of a six-cylinder car engine to describe it. Over the course of my consulting career, I realized that a really high performing private sector company fires on four or five of the six cylinders available in their corporations. CEOs like to think their companies fire on all six cylinders but it isn't true. There are always inefficiencies built into any business model. Too much capacity and capability in most companies are either not critical to the core value delivery mission of the organization, or not operating at full efficiency, or both. Any organization that can regularly fire on four or five of its six operating cylinders is doing pretty well. My experience working in the public sector suggests that government agencies are lucky if they fire on three or four out of six cylinders.

Government agency inefficiency is driven primarily by program constraints limiting how agencies can use allocated funds, inability to flexibly deploy resources based on citizen need, and frequent policy changes driven by election cycles. When outsiders come into the public sector with newfound enthusiasm to change how government works, the first thing that hits them once they get their arms around how the current government business model works is that there is little room to do anything new or to change anything that is already going on.

Whether at the federal, state, or community level agency funding comes with political and legislative constraints, making it extremely difficult to do anything but support legacy capabilities and systems. When you actually map the people working in any government agency to the source of funding and associated constraints placed on their activities you quickly realize there is very little discretionary resource to do anything but the existing program work. That would be fine if there was perfect alignment between citizen need, government policies, and agency programs. Unfortunately, that is hardly the case. I will leave the political issues to other authors and stick to discussing government business models. Most government programs have been around for a long time and were created under a policy that may have made sense at the time but has little bearing on current policy objectives. The result is that government agencies at every level of government end up spending most of their re-sources and energy on managing a disparate set of unrelated pro-grams that don't tie to any clear or integrated policy framework.

It took me a while to figure this out when I led a government agency. Like many others wanting to apply business practice within the public sector, I mistakenly assumed that we could change the agency's capabilities to better align with an economic development strategy relevant to the twenty-first century, focusing on innovation and entrepreneurship. I naively thought we could reallocate re-sources and people to a different set of activities necessary to imple-ment our strategy. It quickly became clear that most of the agency's budget and people were hardwired to a set of legacy programs that couldn't be redeployed to higher priority activities. Changing the constraints in too many instances takes a proverbial act of Congress. Not primarily because the good people who worked in the agency didn't want to be flexible or to change, although there was some of that, but mostly because the federal and state dollars that funded the agency constrained us from changing the activities. If we stopped doing what the agency had always done the funds and people would have gone away too. So agency leads are stuck continuing to do work they know isn't the most important or relevant work they could be doing. Every time an agency tries to stop any program and seek the approval to move the funds to a higher priority activity the constituents and stakeholders who benefit from the old program raise up, enlist their legislators, and lean against any change until the leader backs down. Resistance to change is relentless and no de-cision ever made in the public sector is final. The process wears down any but the most committed accidental bureaucrats.

Once any government leader realizes that only three to four of the available six cylinders are discretionary and can be aligned with a new policy agenda, the entire job becomes about getting the most out of and the biggest impact from those three to four cylinders. There must be a better way to run the railroad! As citizens we would be well served if government established the capability to do R&D for new business models. Government needs a business model innovation factory as much if not more than companies in the private sector. Tweaking the current government business model isn't going to work. We need to experiment with new models designed around the citizen. Throwing technology at the current model won't work. We need government leaders willing to carve out the conditions in the real world to design, prototype, and test novel ways to create, deliver, and capture citizen value. We have all the technology we need. It is stubborn organizations built for an industrial era that resist change and trying new approaches that are getting in our way.

A business model innovation factory for the public sector will mitigate the fear and risk of change by demonstrating what new models might look like when tested at a smaller scale in a less threatening connected adjacency. We need to explore and test new government service business models in the real world so we can see how they work and what it would take to scale them. A public sector business model innovation factory would also provide a good view of the implications if we decide to expand new models or a better platform to manage the transformation of the current ones.

All organization leaders must learn how to do R&D for new business models. Nonprofit, social enterprise, school, and government leaders aren't exempt. Business models aren't just for business.

11 R&D for New Social Systems

Perhaps the most important reason for developing common business model language across public, private, nonprofit, and for-profit sectors is that transforming our important social systems (including education, health care, energy, and entrepreneurship) will all require networked business models that cut across sectors. We need new hybrid models that don't fit cleanly into today's convenient industry sector buckets. We already see for-profit social enterprises, nonprofits with for-profit divisions, and for-profit companies with social missions. Traditional sector lines are blurring. We're going to see every imaginable permutation and will have to get comfortable with more experimentation and ambiguity. Economic prosperity and solutions for our big social system challenges requires business model innovation across sectors. Transforming social systems won't happen by actions taken independently within public or private sector silos but by reimagining and experimenting with new social systems that cut across both in order to deliver value to the patient, student, citizen, and consumer.

Just like organizations need to do R&D for new business models to remain competitive in the twenty-first century, communities also need to learn how to experiment with new social systems. Countries, states, and local communities should create the conditions to enable new social system experimentation. Every community should have a business model innovation factory. Tweaking our current social systems won't work. For example, we are not going to create the education and health-care systems we all need and want by making incremental changes to the way these systems work today. We are not going to fix these systems by throwing technology at them either. Technology may help the current systems work more efficiently, but if we want to transform our existing social systems we are going to have to learn how to deploy technology in a more disruptive way.

We don't need small improvements to our current social systems—we need to design, prototype, and test new ones. Just like the imperative for organizations to explore new business models while operating the current ones, the same is true for social systems. We need to explore and test new social systems in the real world while continuing to live within the current ones. Communities need a business model innovation factory that creates the conditions in the real world to enable R&D for new social systems. Communities that are successful at positioning themselves as business model and social system innovation platforms will not only deliver better solutions to their citizens, but will also create more prosperous vibrant local economies that will be magnets for both human and financial capital.

R&D for new social systems requires a lens that cuts across multiple sectors and business models. Social systems are networks comprised of linked business models that have learned how to coexist with each other. Our social systems have evolved over a long period of time, and the roles and business models of all the players within each system have become well-defined and accepted. For example, our health-care system is comprised of several distinct industry sectors, each with its own set of business model rules. Physician practices, hospitals, health insurance, federal and state government, pharmaceutical, medical devices and supplies, drugstores and many other health-care industry sectors each have their own discreet business models and have learned how to coexist with the other players in the broader system. Business model innovation within any industry sector will press against or disrupt the way the broader system currently operates, with implications for the players in every other sector.

If a drugstore chain experiments with a new business model to deliver care beyond filling prescriptions (like CVS has done with its Minute Clinic division) it affects the business models of nearby hospitals and physician practices. If the government creates a new form of public health insurance it affects the business models of private sector insurers and every other player within the system. Transformative change in any one part of the system affects all the others. Business model innovation disrupts not only direct competitors but also disrupts other business models within the broader industry or social system. That is why it is far easier to innovate within the constraints of an organization's current business model. That is why too many business model innovation ideas never make it off of the whiteboard. Business model innovation often requires new capabilities and partners from across traditional industry sectors and significantly changes the way value is created, delivered, and captured across the system. The most interesting business model innovation opportunities cut across industry sector boundaries. Business model innovators are transforming and reinventing their industries. They are market makers, not share takers.

Measure Innovation Outputs

We need more communities to be innovation hotspots for social system transformation. Too much of our public innovation conversation is about invention and not enough of the focus and resource is on business model and social system change. When I see lists of the top innovation locations around the country and the world I can't help but wonder if we are having the wrong innovation conversation. The 2011 Top Innovation Cities report from 2Thinknow ranked the top 100 global innovation cities. I scanned the rankings to see which U.S. cities made the list. While I was disappointed my hometown of Providence, Rhode Island, didn't make the cut, I was pleased to see our neighbor Boston was ranked number one. Two other U.S. cities joined Boston in the top 10: San Francisco ranked second and New York ranked fourth.

If Boston, San Francisco, and New York are the top three U.S. innovation cities why do their economic, education, health care, and energy systems produce the same poor results as cities around the rest of the country? Seems logical to ask if the top ranked innovation cities are delivering more value to their citizens or making more progress on the big social challenges of our time than other cities. What's the point of innovation if not to deliver value and solve real-world problems?

After barely scratching the surface of examining output measures the obvious question is this: If Boston, San Francisco, and New York are the top U.S. innovation cities, why are their poverty rates so high? According to the U.S. Census the poverty rate in Boston is 19.5 percent, San Francisco 11.3 percent, and in New York 21.2 percent. Why are their education attainment levels so low? Census data reveals that the college attainment rate in Boston is 35.6 percent, San Francisco 45 percent, and New York 27.4 percent. If these cities are innovation hotspots and models for the rest of the country shouldn't they deliver better economic opportunity, and better education, health care, and energy solutions, as well as a better quality of life to their citizens? Isn't innovation about delivering value?

Maybe the ranking is really more about invention than innovation. Maybe we are too focused on measuring the inputs of innovation and not the outputs. I believe far too much attention and resources are focused on the inputs versus the outputs of innovation. There are more ideas and new technologies than we could ever use or implement. There are too many inventions stuck in the garage or lab and concepts stuck on the whiteboard. We need to get more ideas and solutions off of the whiteboard and into the real world. The imperative is for real-world experimentation of new business models and social systems. We need to try more stuff to see what works and is scalable. We have the inputs for innovation at our disposal. Our focus needs to shift to the outputs. It isn't an innovation until value is delivered. Innovation should be measured based on outcomes. Are there proof points that the solution works in the real world and at scale? We need to invest more in platforms and tools to enable new business model and system-level experiments. We need to invest in and organize safe zones where we can try new approaches in the real world designed around the end-user.

We have bought into a global invention narrative and haven't been successful at replacing it with a compelling innovation story. Inputs are not as dependent on messy collaboration across silos and organizations as outputs. Inputs are easier to measure than outputs. Most importantly, we are wired to focus on inputs and uncomfortable being held accountable for outcomes. Innovation capacity and metrics need to be more about the outputs.

We are blessed around the world with an incredible concentration of inputs for innovation. We must develop an innovation story that is about better outputs and solutions. Why not organize our community innovation strategies to deliver real transformation in our health care, education, energy, and entrepreneurship systems? If we did, communities would be better positioned to deliver on the promise of technology for patients, students, entrepreneurs, and citizens. Let's turn communities around the world into innovation hotspots and measure progress based on outcomes.

Education Rant

The idea of doing R&D for new social systems designed around the end-user applies to all social systems, but a good example and place to start would be with education. Talk about a burning platform.

> *"Education is not the filling of a bucket, but the lighting of a fire."*
> —W. B. Yeats

Excuse the rant, but I am outraged by the state of the U.S. education system. We have let the pilot light go out and we are failing our youth. It is time to move beyond public policy debates and institutional rugby scrums to try new systems solutions. What we are doing now isn't working and far too much of the federal stimulus investment is being spent to sustain the current system. Tweaking the current system will not work. Point solutions will not create the results we want and need. We need transformation. We need to experiment with new system solutions designed around the student.

A report from the nonprofit network America's Promise Alliance showed that 1.2 million students drop out of high school each year. Only about half of the students served by school systems in the nation's 50 largest cities graduate from high school. The U.S. public education system, especially in the country's urban centers, must be transformed. Only about 40 percent of the U.S. adult population earns a college degree. That may have been fine in the twentieth century when an industrial economy supplied good jobs to those without postsecondary education. It is not fine today when a postsecondary credential is a necessity for a good job.

Our education system was built for the twentieth century.

Everyone loves to point fingers at the other players in the system as the cause of the problem. Observing our education system today is like watching an intense rugby scrum that is moving in slow motion hoping the ball will pop out. There is finger pointing and incessant public policy debates galore. We love to admire the problems: It's the unions that are getting in the way. Teachers are resisting change in the classroom. Administrators don't understand what is going on in the classroom. Parents are not engaged. Public policymakers can't make up their minds. If only private sector companies were more engaged. Students are unruly, undisciplined, and disrespectful. Everyone is blamed and nothing changes.

The simple idea of "lighting a fire" expressed in Yeat's quote says it all for me. Teaching is an important means to an end. Creating passionate lifelong learners is the objective of education. Content, subjects, jobs, and requirements will all change over time. The pace of change is accelerating and the half-life for assumptions and usable knowledge is decreasing. It has become a lifelong challenge to stay relevant. The only thing that is sustainable is a fire inside to keep learning. The objective of education is to light a fire for learning in every single youth. When the pilot light is on, everything else is possible. For starters, let's recognize that individuals have different learning styles. One-size industrial education models are not working and must be transformed. We have the enabling technology available to us today to create and scale an education system that provides access to killer content and experiential learning opportunities tailored to individual learning styles for every student. It is time to demonstrate that we can and will change our education system. Our youth are waiting.

The same urgent need to transform elementary and secondary school systems exists for higher education systems as well. Colleges and universities are some of the world's most important assets. We need these institutions to enable citizens to be passionate, lifelong learners and doers. We need them to help advance the world's thought capital and catalyze the translation of ideas into solutions. We need them to produce innovators who can solve the big social challenges we face.

Unfortunately, postsecondary education in the United States is stuck in the twentieth century with an industrial-era business model that is both worn at the edges and unsustainable.

We need a much larger percentage than 40 percent of the U.S. adult population to be able to earn that education at a price they can afford. Instead, the price of higher education is out of reach for many, and financial aid models are stretched to their breaking point.

More troubling still, ongoing work at BIF's Student Experience Lab reveals a wide disconnect between the way our country's youth thinks, learns, communicates, and collaborates and the way postsecondary institutions are organized to deliver value to the student.

Nothing short of system transformation will be sufficient to increase student access, enhance their experience, take advantage of the disruptive potential of technology, and improve the quality and cost effectiveness of the U.S. higher education system.

Most economists agree that new venture creation is the lifeblood of a vibrant economy and central to long-term, sustainable job growth. The current economic crisis has only magnified our country's need to stimulate entrepreneurship. But college and university support for entrepreneurs starting new companies, new social ventures, or even just bringing their skills into the workplace is insufficient.

Too many people have bought into the idea that new ventures are a direct result of our national investment in university-based research. The theory goes: Investment in basic and applied research in colleges and universities will create the ideas and technologies that enable entrepreneurs to start the next Google, transform our health-care system, or solve global warming. I have been watching this movie for a long time and it doesn't seem to play out that way.

College and university presidents all say the right things. Speech after speech promote their institutions as hotbeds for entrepreneurship. But when you look behind the scenes at the hallowed halls, you see a very different picture. Research universities are organized around the inputs to innovation. They are designed to maximize the flow of research dollars from government and private-sector sources into the establishment. Academic programs and policies are focused more on technology transfer and licensing opportunities than on creating an environment conducive for students and faculty to experiment with brand new ventures.

We need our country's higher education system to help create a citizenry of passionate, lifelong learners. It should also enable the translation of new ideas and technologies into new ventures, higher wage jobs, and solutions for the big social issues of our time. Tweaking the current system will not work. We need to experiment with new higher education system approaches designed around the student. Wake up, colleges and universities. Tear down those Ivory Tower walls.

To transform the education system we need to create the conditions in the real world to experiment with new business model and system-level solutions. What if we put students in the driver's seat of a new kind of R&D to transform education? What if we created a business model innovation factory for education that provided a platform for engaging students more fully in a real-world effort that also involves teachers, education administrators, and other system players? Could we improve a student's education experience? Could we take it a step further and transform education itself?

Do you remember being stuck at the kids' table for Thanksgiving dinner growing up? I do. There were always too many of us to all sit around one dinner table, so we had a secondary table off to the side, sometimes even in a separate room, to which the younger generation was relegated. I remember asking every year if I would be able to sit with the grown-ups. The conversation at their table ranged from sports to politics to family gossip, and whatever the topic it was always more animated and intense. I know why now: it's because adults love to talk about the state of their world and how it should get better. But what an irony: those of us with the biggest stake in the future, the kids, were not even hearing the conversation. Back then, all I understood was that the main table was where the action seemed to be, and I wanted in.

These days, I do get to sit at some main tables, but I try to stay mindful of whose voices aren't being heard there, particularly when they are young and presumed not to have anything to add. I feel this most acutely in the debates around education reform. We keep kids off to the side while the adults talk and talk and talk about how to improve student experience and outcomes. And there's another similarity to Thanksgiving meals: a lot of loud conversation and not much action! The talk at the grown-up table never stops, yet year after year the education system in the United States continues to atrophy and our students fall further behind the global curve. Every 29 seconds in America another student gives up on school, adding up to nearly a million high school dropouts a year.

What if we put students at the center of the education innovation conversation? Could we get past our suspicion that they would make ignorant or irresponsible suggestions, and tap into what they know better than any of us: what works for them as learners? If we engaged kids in the problems facing schools and gave them access to design tools, they might imagine a learning experience they would be more likely to engage in and commit to. What if we didn't stick our youth at the kid's table?

At BIF, our Student Experience Lab is collaborating with Rhode Island Education Commissioner Deborah Gist and her team at the state's Department of Education on a project with a simple question at its heart: Can students design their own education future if we trust and enable them? We started by convening 40 students aged 12 to 22, who traveled to Providence from all corners of Rhode Island's public education system, to show us. Right at the start of the day it was announced that there would be a kids' table, but guess who was relegated to it? Myself, Commissioner Gist, and all of the other adults in the room, leaving the students at the main tables to drive the conversation while we listened.

Sure enough, just like at the Thanksgivings of my childhood, all the action was at the main table. As the room overflowing with engaged youth began filling flip charts and flip cameras with idea after idea for improving their student experience, we adults were blown away by their purpose and passion. First of all, the session took place on a Saturday: These 40 students were giving up half of a precious weekend to think and talk about school and how to improve it. And their energy level remained high for the entire day.

Perhaps not surprisingly, it wasn't because they hate school. The students made it clear right away that they see the value of school, and given the opportunity to design their dream student experience, not one of the eight student teams argued for throwing out the traditional school model completely. They embraced the importance of a strong core curriculum, but their ideas suggested how hungry they are for the freedom to follow their unique curiosities, and learn skills in the context of subjects that already fascinate them. They also had things to tell us about the importance of learning relationships, and how schools could provide more mentors and role models.

They also told us a few things about how it felt to be at the kids' table. They were aware that no one had ever asked them before what they thought, and that when they did speak up in their various ways, they were not heard. One student remarked, "I come to school to be heard, so shouldn't you listen?"

I'm certain we only scratched the surface of what young people can contribute to the education reform conversation that day. More broadly, think of all the areas where adults are monopolizing a conversation in which youth have the largest stake. We should recognize that young people seek purpose and want to impact their surroundings, including school, but not limited to it. We should listen to and involve youth more in designing any future we have a hand in, but they will inherit.

In addition to designing any new education system for and with students it is important to experiment in a connected adjacency. If we want system change it won't work to design isolated examples of success and hope that the rest of the system adopts the new practice. We have seen this clearly with the charter school movement. There are many examples of charter schools that have had incredible success at transforming the way a school works to deliver better value to the student. Charter schools have demonstrated how to create better outcomes, particularly for students living in U.S. urban centers that have faired particularly poorly in traditional public schools.

Charter schools have sprung up across the country and yet haven't had the broad system impact we need and want in helping to transform our core education system. I believe that is because they were not set up as connected adjacencies. They are isolated from and typically at war with the core system. No surprise the core system has resisted and effectively blocked their expansion. A better model would be to establish the conditions connected to the current system for experimentation of new education models and systems. Like any business model innovation factory it would have to have strong support from community leaders, the autonomy and resources to freely experiment with new system solutions (even those that might disrupt the current system), and a connection to the core system with transparency to enable fluid exchange of ideas and capabilities.

The same approach to system experimentation and change for education should be applied to other social systems including health care, energy, and making entrepreneurship central to our economic future. These are all systems-level challenges that will only be solved with system-level solutions. As much as we think we can or as hard as we try to fix them with incremental changes to the current systems or by throwing new technology at them, it won't work. If we want transformed systems we need to learn how to do R&D for new ones. We need to create the conditions in the real world to experiment with new social systems. Experiments should be designed not through the lens of the current systems and institutions (both public and private) that comprise them but through the lens of the end-user. Use participative design approaches directly involving the student, patient, citizen, and entrepreneur to prototype and test new social system solutions. The way we have been trying to improve social systems isn't working. It is time to try a different approach.

12

What's Your Personal Business Model?

Sometimes tweaks aren't enough. Sometimes nothing short of reinventing yourself is called for. As individuals we have business models too. Each of us has a personal story that develops over time about how as individuals we create, deliver, and capture value. Our personal business model stories are informed by the world around us. Personal business model stories are shaped by input from our environment, families, friends, teachers, coaches, and experiences.

The same patterns we see with organizational business models can also be seen with personal business models. They get stale over time. And in the twenty-first century they get stale faster. Just like all organizations get set in their ways, so do we as individuals get locked into a personal business model. And just like organizations become vulnerable to being disrupted and displaced by new business models, the same thing is true for individuals. If we don't learn how to reinvent ourselves we are at risk of being disrupted. If we don't learn new personal capabilities and new ways to create, deliver, and capture value we risk becoming less relevant over time.

How many people do you know that have been devastated by the current economic downturn? New jobs will be created eventually, but those jobs will require a different set of skills than those that were lost. We will have to get better at changing our personal business models to be ready for the new jobs of the twenty-first century. We will have to learn how to reinvent ourselves. And just like the half-life of any company business model is declining in the twenty-first century, so is the half-life of any personal business model. Business models just don't last as long as they used to. The skills and experiences that have helped us to this point are not the same skills and experiences that will propel us forward. We all are going to have to reinvent ourselves—not just in response to the current economic downturn, but many times over the course of our careers and lives. Business model innovation is imperative for individuals too. One personal business model is not going to last. As individuals we are going to have to explore new personal business models while we are busy pedaling the bicycle of our current one. We must learn to personally experiment with new ways to create, deliver, and capture value in order to stay relevant and to have the personal impact that we aspire to and are capable of.

For starters, we have to rethink the future of work. Today's concept of work, employment, and jobs are an outgrowth of an industrial era that is long gone. The industrial era is not coming back and it is time to rethink the basic concept of work. Despite what politicians say, most of the jobs lost in the current downturn aren't coming back. Work takes on new meaning in the twenty-first century and it is time to change our conversation. The real wake-up call of this downturn is the enormous skill's gap between the requirements of a twenty-first century economy and the skills and experience of the current workforce. Waving our hands and political rhetoric will not close the gap. Our education and workforce development systems must be transformed. Now. The nature of work and the way we think about jobs must change dramatically. As a way to stimulate your thinking, here are a few ideas on the future of work.

- Work becomes more about meaning and impact than repeatable tasks.

- Nine to five is so yesterday.
- Global sourcing goes on steroids enabling third-world opportunity and growth.
- Free Agent Nation becomes a reality.
- Projects are more important than jobs.
- Teams assemble and reassemble based on the job to be done.
- Changing nature of work transforms our daily commute and transportation systems.
- Industrial-era organizations give way to purposeful networks.
- Everything we think and know about professions will change.
- Education is no longer K–16 but a lifelong commitment.
- Workforce and economic development are transformed and become indistinguishable.
- Work becomes more self-organized and less institutionally driven.
- Job titles are more about what you can do than meaningless status monikers.
- Compensation is about performance outcomes, not seniority.
- Entrepreneurship becomes democratized and the key economic driver.
- Work and social life become indistinguishable.
- Getting better faster is imperative.
- Art and design become integral to work and value creation.
- Making things becomes important and interesting again.
- Passion drives meaningful work.

Stay on a Steep Learning Curve

If you want to reinvent your personal business model, become a lifelong learner. Put yourself in environments and accept roles where you can learn the most. The people that are best positioned to reinvent themselves and their personal business models hang out at the edge and force themselves to stay on steep learning curves. It is the only way to ensure constant exposure to new perspectives and experiences resulting in new capabilities and ways to create, deliver, and capture value. Steep learning curves enable personal business model innovation.

Innovators leap across learning curves, exploring new ways to deliver value the way Tarzan swung from vine to vine across the jungle. They thrive on the steepest part of the learning curve where the changing rate of learning is the greatest. Watch how innovators manage their careers and lives. They always put themselves on a steep learning curve. I know I always have. Staying on a steep learning curve is the most important decision criterion for any career decision an innovator makes. Along the way they make many career moves, none of which are primarily about titles, offices, number of direct reports, or money. Innovators believe those things are more likely to happen if they keep themselves on steep learning curves. Every choice to take a new tack or direction is about the next learning curve. Innovators are self-aware enough to know they do their best work while learning at a rapid rate and are bored to tears when they aren't. Steep learning curves matter most.

I have known many people who sacrificed learning curves for money and other extrinsic rewards and in the long run most ended up unhappy. In my experience, innovators who follow their passions and are in it for the learning always end up happier and making more money anyway.

The tricky part is to know when to leap from one learning curve to the next the way Tarzan traversed vines to move through the jungle. Innovators get restless when any curve starts to flatten out. Instead of enjoying the flat part of the curve where it takes less effort to produce more output, innovators get bored and want to find new learning curves where they can benefit from a rapidly changing rate of learning. If the goal for innovators is to get better faster the only way to accomplish it is to live on the edge where the knowledge flows are the richest. It isn't the most comfortable place to be. It's understandable most suffer the pain of the steep part of the learning curve, not for the kick of learning, but to finally reach the flat part of the curve. There is no urgency to move to another curve once the plateau is reached.

It is comfortable on the flat part of the curve where the workload lessens and rewards are only available to those that have paid their dues and put in the time to climb up the curve. Yet innovators seem to extract what they need from the steep part of the curve and leap off to do it again, moving on to the steep part of the next curve just when the effort required to further climb the current curve gets easier.

Innovators are less interested in climbing further up learning curves than jumping from curve to curve. They are like Tarzan (no loincloth jokes please) traveling through the forest by jumping from vine to vine. Innovators learn from each curve and cross-pollinate other curves with their interdisciplinary experiences. Innovators are disruptive to those clinging to a single learning curve. Picture the disruption caused while hanging on to a vine for dear life when Tarzan gives his bone jarring animalistic jungle cry before jumping on and swinging across the jungle, leaping to the next vine. That's how disruption works. Ideas from each learning curve are combined and recombined to create new ways to deliver value and solve problems. Hanging around on a single curve as the rate of learning slows down is no way to get through the jungle. Innovators with the benefit of leaping across learning curves will enable disruption and get through the forest faster. Maybe an innovator's jungle cry, like Tarzan's, would help speed your personal business model innovation process.

Embrace Vulnerability

If you hang around innovators long enough, it's pretty clear they all have a deep-seated confidence in both their ideas and their ability to turn ideas into reality. The best innovators are able to do this on a regular basis, delivering value along the way. To some, they may seem invincible, impervious to the naysayers, roadblocks, and intransigent systems in their way. But I believe that this confidence, however valuable, is not what distinguishes a great innovator. Instead, innovation requires a level of vulnerability with which most are uncomfortable.

Roger Martin, Dean of the Rotman School of Management in Toronto, says the hallmark of an innovator is having a confident point of view combined with the self-awareness that something is always missing. I agree. Neurosis-laced vulnerability is what enables innovators to seek critical input and make the random connections needed to fuel innovation. There is always a better way and innovators open themselves up in order to search for missing puzzle pieces.

Innovators possess the unique capacity to put themselves and their ideas out in traffic, expecting and welcoming an onslaught of direct and hard-hitting feedback. The cliché that innovators have thick skin is true—but it isn't impenetrable armor. It is a semipermeable membrane that enables a free flow of ideas and experiences in both directions. The innovator's vulnerability enables an active osmosis of ideas, allowing for freely flowing input from diverse external networks.

Don't mistake vulnerability for weakness. Innovators are not weak. They are driven to find a better way and will stop at nothing to find solutions and deliver value. They are not afraid to assert and defend their point of view or present their case for change with confidence and conviction. They don't hold back—and if you listen closely, it's always personal.

Innovators don't give presentations. Instead, they share stories, designed to create an emotional connection with the listener. The stories are often self-deprecating, laying bare the innovator's vulnerabilities. And innovators are central characters in their own narrative, not removed from the process. They're sensitive, too. They're the first ones to read the reviews. They can't wait for feedback and devour every press mention, blog post, or social media blurb. Critiques can't come fast enough, and good, bad, and ugly comments are all welcome. Anything with the potential to improve an idea or concept is welcome insight. Critical feedback from respected sources is the best fuel source.

Innovators celebrate their vulnerability by diving into the gray area between disciplines, sectors, and departments. They know you can't learn anything by being the smartest person in the room or from hanging around with people who all think and act alike. Instead, their goal is to recognize patterns and connect dots horizontally across silos. Connecting unusual suspects by bridging perspectives, language, and approaches is imperative.

Don't mistake vulnerability for naiveté, either. True innovators are firmly grounded in reality and will not claim victory until value is delivered or a problem is solved. Optimism and belief in a better way provides immunity from the anti-everything crowd. A cacophony of detractors is nothing but white noise to an innovator. Despite being surrounded by skepticism and those supporting the status quo, innovators manage to remain positive and committed to their visionary paths forward. Being genuinely vulnerable is in short supply these days. Perhaps it's not a coincidence innovators are such a rare breed.

Blessing and a Curse

Being an innovator is both a blessing and a curse. Innovators are constantly seeking to improve things by finding a better way. A questing personality is a blessing, providing innovators with a source of personal pride, accomplishment, and exhilaration. At the same time, an innovator's job is never done. There is always a better way. A sense of perpetual incompleteness and never being satisfied torments most innovators I know. I think this blessing and curse dichotomy is the secret sauce that makes innovators tick. It motivates innovators to take personal risks, collaborate with unusual suspects to find a missing piece, and jump through incredible hoops seeking a better way. Innovators wouldn't have it any other way.

There is always a better way. It doesn't matter how innocuous or small a thing from everyday life it is. You can always tell an innovator because they fixate on addressing small things with the same childlike enthusiasm they readily deploy to large complex societal problems. It's the little things that often get innovators the most riled up.

I learned this lesson the hard way and share one of many personal examples. After a long career as a road warrior strategy consultant I found myself at home trying to figure out what I was going to do next in my career. One morning I came downstairs and opened the cupboard that housed breakfast cereal for our three children and found it filled with 12 half-opened cereal boxes. You know the one I am talking about. Tell me you can't relate to this important dilemma. I fell into the trap and loudly proclaimed, "Isn't there a better way to organize this cereal?" The response was immediate and resounding, thanks for the input, now go find something else to do, preferably out of the house! I know my wife is groaning reading this thinking, no, not the cereal box story again. Can't you come up with a new story for heaven's sake? (P.S. regarding the cereal box story, the children and the cereal boxes have left home and I miss them both terribly.)

Innovators can't help themselves, no matter how small the challenge; there is always a better way and they are driven to find it. It's not just the small things. If you are like me it bugs you enough to create new solutions in your head while stuck in an avoidable traffic jam when the information was knowable, when one part of the health-care system has no clue of your experience with the rest of it, and when one government agency has no visibility to your history with the agency right next door. Don't even get me started on education because it just makes me cry. It is inconceivable to me how we have let our public school systems atrophy to their current state. All of the innovators I know are outraged, screaming for transformational change, and willing to roll up their sleeves and help design a better way.

Innovators are constantly deconstructing life experience and coming up with new approaches to delivering value and solving everyday problems. It is rarely about inventing anything new. Innovators often solve problems with existing technology and by recombining capabilities in new configurations to deliver value in a better way. Innovators are blessed to see a bigger picture, enabling a larger palette from which to paint new solutions.

Innovators are also cursed by never being satisfied. The job is never done. Celebrations are muted and short-lived as innovators move on to explore the next better way. Ignorance is never bliss to an innovator. There is always a missing piece of information that torments innovators and keeps them up at night until they find it. And when they think they have a bead on it, two more compelling questions arise and the constant quest continues. Innovators are generally anxious people who feed their anxiety by moving toward the edge, where the best knowledge flows are. Innovators are perpetually exhausted, not wanting to miss an opportunity to advance an idea, connect with someone who can help, or find that missing piece of information. It is a curse that innovators gladly accept and have reconciled themselves to live with. Innovators are never satisfied and incredibly hard on themselves, but they are convinced in their souls that seeking a better way is both noble and right. Being an innovator is both a blessing and a curse.

What is your personal business model and how prepared are you to reinvent it?

About The Author

Saul Kaplan is the founder and Chief Catalyst of the Business Innovation Factory.

Kaplan started BIF in 2005 with a mission to enable collaborative innovation. The nonprofit is creating a real world laboratory for innovators to explore and test new business models and system level solutions in areas of high social importance including health care, education, entrepreneurship, and energy independence.

Prior to focusing on business model and system level innovation at the Business Innovation Factory Kaplan served as the Executive Director of the Rhode Island Economic Development Corporation and as the Executive Counselor to the Governor on Economic and Community Development. Kaplan created Rhode Island's unique innovation @ scale economic development strategy aimed at increasing the state's capacity to grow and support an innovation economy, including an effort to turn the state's compact geography and close knit public and private sector networks into a competitive advantage.

Prior to his state leadership role in economic development Kaplan served as a Senior Strategy Partner in Accenture's Health & Life-Science practice and worked broadly throughout the pharmaceutical, medical products, and biotechnology industry. Kaplan also spent eight years working for the Pharmaceutical Division of Eli Lilly and Company. As a Marketing Plans Manager, Kaplan assisted in developing the launch strategy and successful introduction of Prozac into the U.S. market.

Kaplan shares his innovation musings on Twitter (@skap5), his blog (It's Saul Connected) and as regular contributor to the *Harvard Business Review*, *Fortune* and *Bloomberg Business Week*.

Kaplan holds an MBA from Rensselaer Polytechnic Institute focusing on the strategic management of technology and a BS in Pharmacy from the University of Rhode Island.

Index